For my dear parents, Priya and Padmakar, whose love and kindness has shaped who I am.

Your Free Gift

I'd like to give you a gift as my way of saying thanks for purchasing this book. It's my mini ebook titled **10 Steps to Reinvent Yourself**. It provides tips on how to transform yourself and lead a more fulfilled life. It will help you immensely.

You can get immediate access to the ebook by clicking on the link below.

https://yugeshmandvikar.gr8.com/

Maximum Results

Unlock Your Hidden Abilities, Overcome Your Past, Break Mental Barriers, And Get What You Want in Life

Yugesh Mandvikar

http://yugeshmandvikar.com/

Copyright

Contents

COPYRIGHT 2

YOUR FREE GIFT 4

INTRODUCTION 8

PART I – THE PARADIGM OF SUCCESS 13

   1. Our Foundational Beliefs 14
   2. We Want it "As of Yesterday" 24
   3. Why Do Results Escape Us...33

PART II – THE ANATOMY OF FAILURE 49

   4. The Inner Workings of the Brain 50
   5. Why Setbacks Are Helpful 59
   6. Addressing the Fear of Failure 73

PART III - GETTING UNSTUCK 85

   7. Letting Your Past Be Your Past 86
   8. Moving Beyond our Reasons 97

PART IV – THE MAXIMUM RESULTS METHOD 109

   9. Embarking on The Voyage 110
   10. Focusing Your Attention 117
   11. Creating Powerful Intentions..................................132
   12. Generating Energy of Emotions 146
   13. Leveraging Your Intuition 161
   14. Taking Massive Action 176

CONCLUSION 192

DID YOU ENJOY READING MAXIMUM RESULTS?........196

ABOUT THE AUTHOR 197

A NOTE ON ATTRIBUTION OF SOURCES 198

You were born with potential.

You were born with goodness and trust.

You were born with ideals and dreams.

You were born with greatness.

You were born with wings.

You are not meant for crawling so don't.

You have wings.

Lean to use them and fly.

\-   Rumi

Introduction

The greatest quest of humans is that of their untapped potential.

No matter where you go in this world, there is one thing that you will find in common: the innate desire of people to make their lives better. For millennia, the human species has evolved and continues to do so because of this very desire. The need to grow and go beyond our current frontiers has helped us achieve feats such as landing on the moon and exploring deep seas, which were once inconceivable. This quest to achieve and the indomitable spirit backing it distinguish us from the other species. You reading this book is an indication of your quest to make your life better.

A lot has been said and written about achievement over the last few decades. Since our early childhood, we have been taught about two core tenets, working hard and being humble. There is nothing wrong with these virtues, and arguably these are required to achieve results. Yet a lot of people strive and fail. It is not as if they don't work hard enough, or they lack the key skills required to achieve the results. Somehow, success eludes them. In the case of some others, they achieve some results and remain happy with what they get, while the rest of the opportunities wait to be unlocked someday. People spend their lifetime continuing to expect different results by doing the same thing over and over again.

Time and again, we have witnessed important discoveries and phenomenal breakthroughs. What led to such extraordinary results? Albert Einstein famously said, "We cannot solve our problems with the same thinking we used when we created them." This principle applies similarly to the results we create. You, too, can create something extraordinary. You, too, can create maximum results. What you need is a distinct approach.

This book came to be written after years of observation and study. By virtue of working as a performance consultant and a success coach, I had the opportunity to consult with, train, work with, and coach thousands of individuals and teams. I keenly observed behaviors, actions, and thought patterns, which I have thoroughly enjoyed from my early days.

I had the privilege of witnessing their successes and, more importantly, their failures. Their problems and questions gave me insights. I started noticing the results that people achieved and what they did to achieve them. After years of intent observation, patterns started emerging. The presence of some "things" led to the achievement of results. And not just any results, but extraordinary ones. I have aligned and articulated these patterns into a framework that forms the core of this book. The words "process," "structure," "method," and "framework" have been used interchangeably in this book. I have personally used this model in my own life and reaped benefits. This book itself is a cherished outcome of the application of this model.

The key principles and concepts detailed in this book come from my interactions, observations, and reflections over the last decade and a half, as well as research in the field of neuroscience, behavioral science, psychology, philosophy, leadership, and physics. These are easy to understand, remember and implement, and you can apply them to achieve your desires across any walks of life.

The goal of this book is to help you create maximum results in your life, with winning in mind. You can treat this book as a reference guide, a handbook, or a manual for working on any area of your choice. My experience of working with thousands of people has shown that when you follow up your actions with reflection, you elevate your chances of taking better subsequent action. This goes on, building a loop. You can achieve success through stillness. I have included many reflection exercises in the book, and I invite you to do them without fail. These will solidify your success. My sincere hope is that this book will inspire and help you in taking massive action.

The book is structured in four key parts.

In Part I, we will explore some of our key beliefs around success and the factors that lead to the achievement of results. We will uncover the key reasons why people don't succeed despite working hard for it. We will also understand how we end up sabotaging our success without even knowing it.

Part II reviews the mechanisms of our brain that influence our results. We will understand what happens inside us when we experience setbacks and learn ways of overcoming them. We will explore ways to conquer self-doubt and the fear of failing, which stops us from reaching our full potential.

In Part III, we will prepare the field before we sow the seeds. We will understand how our past influences us and impacts our future and explore techniques for breaking these patterns. The subsequent chapters will guide us in breaking through our inner barriers.

We will explore the Maximum Results framework in Part IV. The framework consists of five dimensions, each of which has been detailed in the chapters with useful tools and techniques for implementation.

Brian Tracy once said, "The great breakthrough in your life comes when you realize that you can learn anything you need to learn, to accomplish any goals that you set for yourself. This means there are no limits to what you can be, have, or do."

You chose to invest yourself in this book. Let this be your breakthrough. You have taken the first step. You have also established and communicated an intention that you want your life to positively change. You have expressed your desire to achieve outstanding and unimaginable results. Will it require focused and guided effort? Surely yes! But you have already started, and that is key.

To endless possibilities!

With a lot of love and light.

Part I – The Paradigm of Success

"The road to success and the road to failure are almost exactly the same."

- Colin R. Davis

1. Our Foundational Beliefs

Sometimes You Do, Sometimes You Don't

The thought of a hot coffee on a summer afternoon was not enticing at all, however, the look on Ashton's face could not make me say no to him. We took a stroll, holding our coffee cups in hand, as he moved his hands vigorously while talking. Someone watching us even from a considerable distance could predict the agitation and tenseness in the conversation. Ashton's face had turned red, not because of the harsh summer sun but the eruption of his frustration. The floodgates had opened with my asking a question. I had just started working with Ashton as his Coach the week before. I was patiently hearing him out as we walked through the central lawns of the building. And at one point, he stopped, looked at me, and said, "Everything was the same. I did exactly what I had done the last time. But it did not work. It just did not work." He shook his head in disbelief as he said, "I don't know why."

One of the most famous folk tales from *Arabian Nights* is that of Aladdin – the boy who had a magical lamp. A genie would appear when the lamp was rubbed. The genie held magical powers to make the wishes of his master come true, every single time without fail. A lot of us have secretly wished for the magical lamp in our lives. Something which will ensure certainty in getting us what we want, every single time.

We have all grown up hearing from our parents, teachers, and significant elders that our hard work is the lamp and you are the genie yourself. You can make it happen; you can work hard to grant all your wishes. Generations after generations have grown up hearing fables and quotes emphasizing the same learning. And it is true! I, too, believe in it. But there is a catch. The problem here is the inconsistency of results with this approach. The reality for most people is far from the fable. The genie escapes us sometimes.

Let's do a small exercise.

Step 1: I invite you to list your last five successes which were important to you. These can be your achievements from any walks of your life, no matter how big or small. (e.g. getting promoted, winning an award, buying the house of your dreams, becoming a parent, etc.)

Step 2: Write down what did you do to achieve your success for each of these five. (e.g. you worked hard, burned the midnight oil, dedicated your weekends, learned the new skills, etc.)

Step 3: List your last five disappointments, areas where you did not get the results that you wanted.

Step 4: Map the reasons listed in step 2 for each of the five disappointments to check if you did any of those but still did not get the results as expected.

The chances are that you would have worked hard even for the areas where you encountered a disappointment, but the outcomes were not in your favor. Like Ashton, all of us have achieved some things and let some things go.

The Success Equation

Generations of women and men have grown up listening to adages telling them what they need to do to succeed in their lives. As Gordon Hinckley put it, "Without hard work nothing grows but weeds." This wisdom still guides our efforts to some extent. As years pass by, elements such as intelligence start gaining prominence. To simply put it in the form of an equation, when one had intellect (ability) and worked hard enough (effort), it was believed to lead to success.

$$Ef \times Ab = Su$$

$$(Effort \times Ability = Success)$$

More than a century ago, Sir Francis Galton, a psychologist of the Victorian era proposed in his book *Hereditary Genius* that achievement required intelligence, as well as zeal and the capacity for hard labor. Charles Darwin, in a letter to Galton, agreed that cognitive ability must matter but added, "I have always maintained that, excepting fools, men did not differ much in intellect, but only in zeal and hard work; and I still think this is an eminently important difference." And so, another trait was added to the equation, that of Passion.

$$Su = f (Ef, Ab, Pa)$$

Success became a function of Effort, Ability, and Passion.

Theorists, scholars, consultants, and scientists have dedicated years of effort to find out what leads to success. Various studies and experiments have been conducted in this area over the past few decades and various theories have been proposed around what leads to success. While there are many takes on it, there is no single right or wrong equation. While there is always a significant focus on hard work and ability, one may argue the influence of elements such as luck, circumstances, family background, and the quality of education to name a few. And the equation can continue to expand, considering many contributing variables.

Success = function of (n1, n2, n3,....,nx)

While the influence of these factors can be debated, let us ask ourselves a key question. Will two individuals who have equal intellectual capacity, have similar backgrounds, and work equally hard always succeed similarly? The chances are likely to be no. A significant focus of what we hear about success is the presence of certain attributes. We often overlook the method used to succeed. Let me explain what I mean by method, through an example. Let us look at a scenario of 2 swimmers. Both are of similar height, weight, and body structure. Both of them have learned swimming techniques at the same swimming institute. Given this data, will both complete a butterfly stroke lap in the same amount of time? Probably no, because each one of them may have developed their unique method of doing things, which in turn also influenced their results.

Success is not always a function of your ability, hard work, and perseverance only. The method you pursue is a key determining factor in the achievement of results.

Point for Reflection

- List the traits that you think are important for success.
- Identify the reasons why you think these traits are important and write them down.

This or That

Before we pursue the discussion on the method any further, it is important to put to rest all thoughts on factors leading to maximum results. Time and again in my coaching conversations, I have observed that people tend to compare their achievements with those of their peers and friends, usually those who are doing better than they are. They cite reasons like, "But she could go to Stanford. My parents could not afford it," or "He ends up being at the right place at the right time. He is just lucky." And these explanations are often cited by professionals who themselves are doing very well in their careers and life. I usually ask them to think about the relationship between these stated reasons and the results. These may have a role to play, but are they the actual reason? Is it Causality or Correlation? The usual response from them is a long reflective pause.

Correlation and Causality may seem deceptively similar, however it is the difference between them that changes the paradigm. Understanding this difference can help people become liberated from their reasons, similar to the ones we explored above. Causation essentially means a cause and effect relationship – the presence of X causes Y to happen. Let us understand this with an example. Jerry has an allergy to peanuts. Every time Jerry eats peanuts, he gets a skin rash. Here, eating peanuts is the cause and the effect of it is a skin rash.

Correlation, on the other hand, simply implies a relationship between two variables. Let us look at another example. An ice cream shop monitors the temperature each day and tracks the sale of ice cream on that day. They have realized, looking at the data, that the warmer the weather becomes, the higher the sale of ice cream. This can be attributed to a positive correlation between temperature and the sale of ice cream. Similarly, a negative Correlation would indicate that there is no relationship between the two variables.

What can we infer out of all of this?

The presence of certain factors such as good education, right opportunities at work, family background, etc. can have a positive correlation to success, but it does not necessarily cause it. Not every individual who had all these factors made significant achievements in life.

The Goal of Goals

"So, what are your resolutions for this year?" Ana asked, quipping with a smile. We were at my friend's house for a lunch get-together to celebrate the New Year. It was the cold winter afternoon of 2009, and we had all decided to gather around a table on the deck to enjoy the sun and the food simultaneously.

"None," I exclaimed.

"How can you and why?" she investigated with surprise. Creating resolutions was like a yearly ritual for her, to be followed no matter what.

"It doesn't work. I know it, and you know it too," I claimed for my retribution. "It stays with you for a couple of days and then fizzles out."

The silent nod told me Ana had been there too. A lot of us have been there. Every year we set goals for ourselves at the start of the year, with a lot of enthusiasm. But then things don't move forward for some reason.

Contemporary wisdom tells us that the best way to achieve something is to set a goal. Whatever you want in life – from getting a promotion to buying a house, finding a soulmate to going on a vacation, wanting to retire early to saving big bucks – create a goal for it. The goals need to be measurable so that we know we are making progress. And when we make progress, we feel motivated to go further and achieve it. The logic is simple and straightforward. But what happens when we don't move forward for any reason? Where would the motivation to continue come from?

Are goals useless? No. Is setting goals a waste of time? Not at all. Goals are helpful. They help us identify *What* we want to achieve. But the absence of a strong *Why* and a clear *How* can lead to outcomes similar to that of New Year resolutions. We create them, and then the next year comes and the cycle repeats itself.

So, what is the secret of goal achievement? A well-set goal by itself cannot provide the stimulus or force for you to overcome your inertia to move ahead. You need a system that will help you make progress. If you want to complete a 10k marathon, you may set a goal for yourself with a date in mind. But just setting this goal will not make you ready to complete the marathon. You need to find a coach, train for endurance, practice running, plan your diet, monitor your key parameters, amongst many other things. This is your system, or method, to achieve the goal. It is important to note that a system and plan are not the same. A system is a macro approach that you follow to achieve what you want. A plan is a specific set of actions that emerge out of the system. I have observed that people who achieved what they wanted, as well as people who did not, all had robust goals. The difference in results was due to the presence or absence of a robust system.

2. We Want it "As of Yesterday"

The Myth of Overnight Success

When I was growing up, I recollect watching an advertisement for a very popular brand of noodles. They claimed to be ready in just 2 minutes. You could enjoy your favorite noodles without any wait. Another ad jingle of a washing machine implied that your clothes could get washed, dried, and ready even before you could finish your tea. From instant water heaters to instant mortgages, nowadays everything is claimed to happen within the blink of an eye.

As a species, we have grown to hate waiting. We dislike queues because they make us wait. We enjoy our on-demand entertainment systems because we don't have to wait for the commercials to end. The rise of McDonald's is a testament to the concept of "fast food" because people don't have time to sit and eat a lengthy lunch. Our freeways ensure we don't waste time waiting for signals to go green. We live in a world of instant gratification.

There is nothing wrong with not wanting to wait in queues or getting to eat your food quickly. We have been hearing for ages "Time is a precious commodity" or "Time is money." The issue with this mindset is the inherent expectation to get results on everything without waiting. We keep hearing stories of people and celebrities who become "overnight successes" and secretly - deep within our hearts - we wish it could happen to us, too. The proliferation of social media and its increased accessibility have enabled us to take a sneak peek into the lives of others without getting up from our couches. And what do we see? Stories of quick success, flamboyance, riches, and luxury flood the platforms. What you see is what people want you to see. Increased exposure to social media leads to a lot of comparisons. People tend to compare their lives and circumstances with what they see of others, which most of the time is curated. A quick check for you is to go through your own social media accounts. Look at the images that you have posted. Aren't they the best reflection of you and your life right now?

Recent research conducted by the University of Pennsylvania established the causal link between the use of social media and negative effects of well-being, primarily depression, due to these constant social comparisons. While we can temper our social media usage, it is important to assess its impact on our expectations for ourselves and our lives. We may witness stories about businesses and people who became an overnight success, but the truth is that success requires its journey. It takes its own time and effort. This reality needs to set in.

Too Much, Too Fast, Too Soon

From crash diets to get-rich-quick schemes, our world today is full of enticing promises. The allure is strong, yet you must fight your urge to give in. The potential consequences of these urges can be many and grave.

- Nothing is good enough – Today you have a desire and you work hard towards achieving it. Let's assume that you do end up achieving it. Then what? "What's next?" is the question that springs to mind. The novelty of this achievement of yours will soon wear off and you will start looking for a new allure.

- The transience of desire – All of us want things in our life. You may also have identified a thing or two. Most likely, it may be inspired by what someone else, such as a friend, a colleague, a person you admire, or a celebrity, has achieved. Let's say tomorrow that person moves on to something different, bigger and larger. Would you still want to pursue your current goal? The chances are no. You may be influenced to also look at the new goals.

- Lack of preparation – In the zeal to make it to the waters, you may forget to pack for the seas. Every pursuit requires meticulous planning. To fulfill the desire for quick outcomes, one may end up taking shortcuts without thinking through the consequences.

- Oversight of the skills - Success happens when you keep an eye on the future while continuing to work on your present. When you hop from one desire to the other, you may tend to oversee the investment that you need to make in yourself to prepare yourself for the future.

- Emotional wellbeing – FOMO, or the fear of missing out, has been one of the key issues which has emerged due to the rise of social media. The anxiety and fear generated by the thought that others might be living lives better than yours can lead to feelings of envy and can significantly affect self-esteem.

Just About Right

Think of an act that you do almost every day. Often you do it multiple times a day. While you may get better at it, you can never be sure of it. The moment you become sure, it becomes something else. Can you guess what is it?

Whether you may have arrived at the answer or not, you may have certainly assessed my limited prowess of creating riddles. The answer is "estimating." The word "Estimate" originated from the Latin word "aestimatus" which meant "determining the value of." In today's world, we understand estimation as an act of roughly calculating something, an approximation of sorts.

The estimation has always fascinated me. I have been a witness to many conversations where leaders and managers have demanded and presented "accurate estimates" and have asked each other questions like, "Are we sure about this?" Apart from being amused by these oxymoronic conversations, I have always found the trait of balance in estimation very interesting. When you go beyond, you overestimate. When you limit, you underestimate. What is needed is to be just right? This balancing act of estimation has its place in the success journey, especially when you try to achieve success under stress.

- Don't underestimate the effort – A common phenomenon amongst mountain climbers and marathon runners is that often they are forced to abandon their pursuit mid-way. The culprit is an underestimation. Time and again, the human race has witnessed significant failures just because the effort was not estimated correctly.
- Don't overestimate your capacity – Empires have fallen, and reigns have ended because people overestimated their strength,

abilities, and influence. Confidence should not be confused with overestimation of capacity. There is a fine line of difference between the two, which becomes evident with high self-awareness.

As we wade through heaps of information coming our way and the urge to have everything right now, it is important to keep these two signposts in view. While these two factors may look like the two sides of the same coin, they are distinct. The presence of one does not necessarily lead to the other. However, even one of these can derail the results.

One may think, how can we be sure of the estimates that we draw of ourselves? Estimating the exact effort requires us to have done it multiple times. Estimating your exact capacity requires a high level of self-awareness. Both have an element common to them: Experience, the currency of which is time. While they say some things come only with time, I am not proposing that you wait for that wisdom to come to you and only then start on your pursuit. Reflection is a powerful tool that can help you traverse vast expanses of time. A quantum of years with a lack of reflection is just time passing by. Hours of effort followed by conscious reflection can lead to insights worth decades of experience.

The Bitter Truth

I have noticed a funny pattern. Every time I visit a toy shop, I have seen or heard at least one child crying. This day was no different. As I was moving across aisles in Hamleys to look for a toy for my niece, a wail indicated the presence of a disgruntled toddler somewhere around. The loud wail was accompanied by hushes and consoling words by the mother. As I moved to the next aisle, there he was, a little boy holding a Spiderman figure tight. Tears rolling down his cheeks. "But you did not finish your dinner for two days. We had agreed to get you the toy if you finished your dinner," his mom put forth in logic. "Why should I get you the toy?" she asked. "Because I drank milk both the days and I am your son," he retorted. His logic was adorable. His mother, embarrassed by the loud wailing, lifted him and walked out. The little Spiderman fan continued to demand, "I have to have it."

We all believe that we should have some things in life. We pay taxes with the expectation that we will have civil facilities made available to us. We behave like good citizens expecting that the Government will take care of us. But the belief that you should have something just because of who you are is a sense of entitlement. It is important to understand the distinction between rights and entitlement. When you expect that you should get what you want because of who you are, what you have done, or what you have been through in life, it takes the shape of entitlement.

In one organization, I observed many young, bright women and men who had completed their MBA from premier business schools and had joined this company. Like an elite squad, they took to tasks and poured ideas into meetings with the business leaders. After a few months, the enthusiasm dipped, and their disappointment was evident. No one was paying attention to them. Their perspective, which was built while they were in the MBA program, was that they were the best in the industry and companies would fight tooth and nail to have them on board. A sense of entitlement had set in their minds. They approached their managers and business leaders with that mindset and a chip on their shoulders. Their audience ignored their suggestions on the grounds of being impractical and lacking experience.

When someone perceives that she or he should have something because they are better than others, they have a sense of entitlement. When someone perceives that she or he should have something because they had to deal with unfortunate circumstances in the past, this perception has an ingrained sense of entitlement. Whether it is the toddler who feels that his parents owe him the toy or the young MBA's who feel that the managers owe them respect, it is very easy to fall into this trap.

The reality is that the world owes you nothing. When you approach your goals and desires with this mindset, you will do everything it takes for you to get it. You will work against all odds and swim against all tides to make it happen. And that is very empowering. Reclaim your heart.

3. Why Do Results Escape Us

The Perils of Success and Failure

Time after time, I have seen countless women and men struggle with achieving their desired results. They work hard and put in a lot of time and effort to achieve their desires and goals. Three key issues come to the fore.

1. Sometimes, people just get what they want. And that is great, isn't it? I would disagree. Every success has a method to it. For you to replicate or amplify the success, you need to know the method and get better. When people achieve their results in the absence of a method or a process, that becomes their process to approaching goals and desires. While this lack of structure and method may work for some, it is too dependent on external variables. No one can predict which way the ball will bounce.

2. People get happy when they achieve their results. One may argue, "What is wrong with that?" Some may even question the strength of the argument to put this forth as an issue. The premise here is that if you can have a bounty, why get happy with a dollar. Our desires become limited by our mental models and beliefs of what we think we can

achieve. These models and beliefs are created based on our past experiences of effort and achievement – how much effort we put in and what we achieved in return. Why settle for mediocre results, if you have the potential for an unimaginable breakthrough?

3. People's failures become a part of their narrative. They may give up too soon or not try again the next time an opportunity arises. The shadows of past failures loom over to stop the person from taking any action. This, coupled with the lack of structure or process as mentioned in point 1, breeds a lack of clarity – "I don't know what else to do." We will explore this facet in detail in the next part of the book.

You may be left thinking how to get what you want in life. If you consider the three factors listed above, you may feel that you are doomed either way, whether you succeed or fail. Let me assure you that it is not that gloomy. It is quite the opposite. While this exploration may push you to the limits and to question your fundamental approach towards achieving anything, it is worth taking this arduous journey. You will emerge at the end of the tunnel with a structure and a process to achieve your desires in life. And this will be with you for the rest of your life. The process is replicable, which means that you will be able to apply it in many walks of life, to any of your goals and desires, no matter how big or small.

What Comes in the Way?

While working as a Performance Consultant, I noticed recurring patterns amongst people who did not complete their pursuit. Irrespective of the backgrounds of these individuals or the goals they pursued, there were seven key reasons due to which they failed to achieve the results that they wanted. Six out of these were conscious reasons. As the category suggests, one is or can be aware of how this reason is getting in the way. The seventh reason, which we will explore in the next section, is a subconscious one. I have observed that people are often not aware of the existence of that reason and how it impacts them. It requires consistent effort and practice to move that reason from the realm of the subconscious to conscious knowing. But for now, let us look at the six conscious reasons.

Reason # 1 – Lack of Belief

We have heard the three words 'Is it possible?" in our head time and again. While individuals aim for mega goals, they tend to question their ability or the possibility of the attainment of the goal. When this happens at the start of the pursuit, the individual may drop their arms, thinking that it is not worth putting in the effort. When this questioning happens in the middle of the journey, the individual may just give up and retreat. One of the most effective ways to overcome the lack of belief is to look at some of your past successes and remind yourself that you have succeeded in the past. Affirmations can also be powerful tools to instill belief and confidence in one's own abilities.

Reason # 2 – Getting Stuck in *How*

Often, the lack of answers to "How will I achieve this" overpowers the drive for the achievement of goals. The lack of knowing slowly takes the shape of impossibility and feeds the lack of belief, mentioned above in reason # 1. People get stuck in the *How* maze and find it difficult to come out. They find it difficult to get unstuck. Reminding yourself that *How* follows only after *What* and *Why* can help you manage the anxiety of not knowing all the answers. Conducting research, finding a mentor, speaking to other people who have done it or in the process of it, can be some of the other actions which can help you.

Reason # 3 – Procrastination

The word comes from the Latin word "Procrastinatus," which is a combination of the prefix "pro," meaning "forward," and "crastinus," meaning "of tomorrow." Procrastination is better understood as putting away or delaying tasks that you know you should do today. People also describe it as inner inertia that keeps them from acting. Often, people procrastinate because the outcomes are not important enough for them. One of the ways to overcome procrastination is to make the outcomes so important that you cannot even think of keeping the actions away. Find the reasons why your goals are important for you and instill them deep within you.

Reason # 4 – Being Overwhelmed
Imagine standing in front of the Willis Towers (or Sears Towers, as it was previously known) in Chicago. The sheer scale of the building overpowers you and leaves you in awe. Some of our pursuits incite a similar feeling within us. We stall, feeling overwhelmed by the scale of the task. A very effective way to deal with being overwhelmed is to break the problem into smaller, manageable pieces. Remember the analogy of eating the turkey. You cannot eat the whole turkey in one go. You must first cut it into bite-sized pieces. Once you break down the problem, take up a couple of smaller pieces and work on them.

Reason # 5 – Distractions
We live in a digital world. Every minute, hundreds of millions of emails are sent, millions of search queries are run, and millions of videos, posts, and pictures

are uploaded on the internet. We swim through this deluge of information and at times get swept away in the tides of social media, misplacing our sense of time. Giving your phone and other gadgets a timeout is one of the ways to manage distractions. Identify a chunk of time every day that you can dedicate to working on your goals. Start by reducing the distractions only for that period and then gradually increase.

Reason # 6 – Too much detail

This reason may be more peculiar to some, due to their personality traits and behavioral preferences. The presence of this reason stops people from moving ahead, until the time they have the minutest of the detail with them. One would agree that in today's world, it may be utopian to know everything about everything before moving ahead. Imagine driving on a dark freeway with no other vehicles around. All you can see in the next 100 or 200 meters is through the headlights of your car. Does it mean that the road beyond those 200 meters does not exist just because you cannot see it yet? No. As you move further, the next 200 meters become visible and then the next 200 meters and so on. Remind yourself of this the next time you are craving more and more details.

Point for Reflection

- Step 1 – Consider your current goals and list them in the table below. You might have made significant progress on them, or you may be stuck somewhere. Irrespective of the current status, list them down.
- Step 2 – For each of the goals, identify if any of the six reasons mentioned above are present. Mark them in the second column.
- Step 3 – Identify the actions that you can take to get unstuck from each of the reasons.

Goal	Presence of Reasons	Possible Actions

How do "You" Get in the Way

We explored six key conscious reasons which impede our growth and actions. Let's now look at the seventh reason. As I had mentioned in the previous section, this reason is subconscious, the presence of which we may or may not be aware.

I call this reason, the Deep Script. A Deep Script is a mental script or a mental model that each one of us has. It defines who you are, how you feel, how you think, what you can do, what is possible, how others perceive you, and many other elements. Essentially it is the script of your life. As in a play, the script defines what happens in each of the scenes, and the characters of the play enact their part per the script. We, too, act per our Deep Scripts.

How Do Deep Scripts Work?

The Deep Script determines how we perceive the world and, in turn, how we perceive ourselves. Your brain encounters massive amounts of data every day. Your experiences, your thoughts, the happenings around, the news, the conversations that you have are just some of them. Your brain interprets each of these data points per your Deep Script. Let me share an example of an individual whom I was coaching.

Jeremy was identified as someone with high potential. However, Jeremy's Deep Script had it that he was not worthy enough. The year prior, Jeremy could not get his due promotion as the company was not doing very well and they decided to defer all promotions. Jeremy, in line with his Deep Script, took that decision as "he was not good enough for the promotion." The incident reinforced his self-perception, and his Deep Script was further strengthened. The subsequent year, Jeremy won an award for an excellent performance. While he seemed happy at the prospect of winning the award, he kept low-key. He brushed the appreciation aside every time someone congratulated him, under the garb of humility. His Deep Script was not allowing him to see himself as worthy of the award. And all of this was happening with Jeremy not even realizing it.

Components of Your Deep Script:

Having a Deep Script is like wearing a pair of colored glasses without even realizing that you are wearing them. Your Deep Script determines your reactions and actions in situations: how you think, how you feel, and, in turn, how you act. Have you ever thought about why certain people are affected by some events much more while others aren't? In behavioral sciences, this is usually qualified as the difference in personality traits and behavioral preferences. Your Deep Script contains these preferences. To put it simply, people respond differently in situations because their Deep Scripts are different. Your Deep Script contains your self-image (how you see yourself and your abilities in terms of what you can and can't do, what you are good at, etc.), your needs, and preferences.

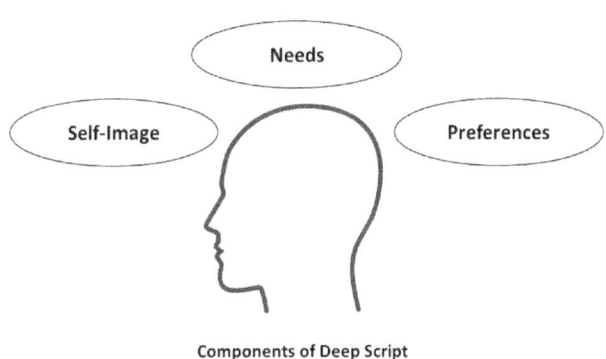

Components of Deep Script

When you choose your goals and desires, this Deep Script is running in the background. It calls out to you whether your goals are too ambitious or achievable. It also prompts when you should take an action and when you should not. People who work to address their procrastination often end up working at a surface behavior level. They take new actions and work towards forming new habits. At times the real action needed is below the surface: addressing their Deep Script.

How Do Deep Scripts Come into Being?

Deep Scripts are created from the early childhood days. Your upbringing and the experiences that you go through in your formative years form the foundations of the Script. These shape the central character of the Script: you. Neuroscience suggests that all the experiences that we encounter from our early childhood days remain stored in our brains. Sometimes we are not able to access them, but those memories remain stored inside.

Over time, the Deep Scripts take a form similar to that of a meta-algorithm that runs the overall program. As you move further on your life, you encounter various experiences. You read and come across a lot of information. You think and reflect. You meet new people and get to hear their perspectives. All of these may influence the Script. It is like a twist in the plot – the events in the life of the central character in a soap opera. Do all such events cast a change in your Script? The degree of influence that an event may have in changing your Script depends on two key factors:

1. The intensity of the experience – If the intensity of the event is high, it will likely generate some strong emotions and make you think or reflect. That, in turn, can make you form new thinking patterns and change the Script.
2. Your level of awareness of both the event and the Script – If your self-awareness is

high, you can see how your Script comes into play in the event and influences your actions. That awareness helps you modify your Script.

Working on your Deep Script:

Don't take it as if the Deep Script is a mental anomaly and we have an issue with ourselves. We all have these Deep Scripts. The key is to be aware of what our Deep Script is and how we can make it work for us, rather than it making us work. You need to find out what parts of your Deep Script are not serving you or are getting in the way. Not all parts of the Deep Script require a change.

It is important to understand how your Deep Script impacts you and how you can use it or change it to your advantage. To do the latter, you need to know what your Deep Script is. While getting to know your complete Deep Script requires you to embark on a self-awareness journey which can take years, you can leverage the power of reflection, supplemented by some short exercises, to know more about your Deep Script.

Exercise 1:

Space: For this exercise, park yourself in a quiet corner of your house. You can also do this exercise outdoors. The only requirement for space is that it should be quiet, and there should be no distractions around.

Time Required: 1 hour (15-20 minutes for completing the instructions and balance; 40-45 minutes for reflection).

Material Required: You need a blank sheet of paper, on which you can draw and write. You also need a pen or a pencil to draw and write. If you have color pencils, that's even better.

Steps for the Exercise:

- Step 1 – Sit in a comfortable position. Relax and center your thoughts. Take 3 deep breaths to calm yourself. Affirm to yourself that you will focus your energy and thoughts completely on this exercise for the next 1 hour.

- Step 2 – Think of some key high points and low points of your life, right from your childhood days. The high points can be significant positive milestones of your life. These can be any events that have been a highlight for you. Similarly, the low points can be events and experiences which were difficult for you in terms of circumstances or results. 2-3 high points and 2-3 low points should suffice for the exercise. Make sure that these are significant in your life.

- Step 3 – Plot these high points and low points on the sheet of paper in the order they happened in your life (from your childhood days to the present day). If you can draw these events on paper using colored pencils, that's even better. Let yourself be free and as creative as you can. You can use words, images, or even icons to depict these events in your life.
- Step 4 – Once you have completed the depiction, take some time to look at the sheet. Be present to the thoughts and feelings that emerge.
- Step 5 – Answer the following questions:
    - What traits can you observe in yourself?
    - How have these events shaped you?
    - Which of your habits, thought patterns, and behaviors can you attribute to these events?
    - Are the resultant habits, thoughts, and behaviors helping you or hindering your progress? And, in what way?

Once you have completed the exercise, keep the answers to the questions in view. Keep visiting them occasionally. The answers to the questions in step 5 can indicate the components of your Deep Script. Remember that, at times, it may take multiple attempts and reflections for things to emerge. Patience and persistence are key.

Exercise 2:

For this exercise, the requirements for space, time, and material are similar to those for Exercise 1.

Steps for the Exercise:

Keep in mind that you need to complete this exercise in a third-person format. This essentially means that you will answer these questions as observations that you have made of a person named you. Your ability to look at yourself in a third-person perspective creates a temporary dissociation between you and your Deep Script. This helps the answers flow naturally and enhances the chances of you getting to know more about your Deep Script.

Step 1: Insert your name in the relevant space in each question. These spaces are marked in the form of < _____ >

Step 2: Relax yourself and take your time to answer the following questions:
   1. Who is < _____ >?
   (E.g. Who is Jim? – Jim is a loving and kind man. He is devoted to his family….)
   2. What is important for < _____ > in life?

3. What are the typical preferences of <_____> in life?

4. Who all have played a significant role in the life of <_____> and how did they shape his/her thoughts?

5. What significant choices did <_____> make in life and how did they shape him/her?

Step 3: Remember, you don't have to complete all the questions in one go. Revisit this worksheet as and when you feel like it and keep adding more. Spend some time reflecting on the answers.

Through these two exercises, patterns will emerge between the reasons for your choices and key events, and people in your life. You will be able to establish a connection. You will have completed a significant step in your journey of awareness. You may not have all the answers with you right now, but you have posed the right questions. Don't worry; the answers will come to you. Keep the faith and move ahead.

Part II – The Anatomy of Failure

"There is only one thing that makes a dream impossible to achieve: the fear of failure."

- Paulo Coelho

4. The Inner Workings of the Brain

The Opposites

You may wonder why we are talking about failures in a book about success. Isn't it the exact opposite? You chose to read this book so that you could achieve what you desire, not how you can lose it. It is precisely the same reason why we are talking about failure. Jerker Denrell of the Stanford School of Business suggests, "Studying successes without also looking at failures tends to create a misleading — if not entirely wrong — picture of what it takes to succeed."

People witness their fair share of successes and failures during their lifetime. However, they don't succeed and fail in isolation. The factors leading to success cannot be completely devoid of the ones leading to failure, and vice versa. They are two sides of the same coin. Past successes may have a bearing on your future successes. Similarly, past failures may influence your choices and actions in the future. Our understanding of success and the factors that lead to it must account for the failures and their impact, too. The study of success is incomplete without the study of failure.

The Seven Fatal Drains

To understand the patterns, failure is defined as "the lack of achievement of desired results." In Part I, we looked at seven key reasons why people don't get the results they aim for. The lack of results comes with disappointment. You also inherit seven fatal drains with the lack of achievement. These seven drains deprive us of our vitality and strength to aim further and pursue any future goals.

Fatal Drain # 1 – The Unanswered Question

The question of "Was it worth it?" plagues many minds. The tendency to question ourselves given the time, effort, energy, and resources that were spent is common. The question is laden with guilt and one may beat oneself up for the loss.

Fatal Drain # 2 – The Dust That Never Settles

When one works incredibly hard and desires the achievement dearly, the lack of success instills a sense of defeat. This sense reverberates inside the mind for a long time without coming to rest.

Fatal Drain # 3 – The Bruised Mind

People report significant fatigue after witnessing the results of failure. Often, this fatigue is not a result of the strain due to the effort put in; it is because of the settling of the news of the results.

Fatal Drain # 4 – The Rise of the Inner Critic

No matter how successful someone may have been in the past, even a small failure can make him or her question themselves. As a result, people end up finding faults in their efforts and abilities.

Fatal Drain # 5 – The Fable of "Never"

Humans are creatures of habit. We inherently gravitate towards repetition. A recent failure may quickly find allies of the past and build up our story of "It never works."

Fatal Drain # 6 – The Calamity of Fate

"I am not lucky," "I don't have it in my destiny to have it," "God does not want me to have it," and many such thoughts flood us at the behest of our mind.

Fatal Drain # 7 – The Sinking Barrel

All of us have a self-view, which is an image and a perception of ourselves. Witnessing a failure in an area in which we were confident of success can have a deep and lasting impact on our self-esteem and confidence.

It's a Jungle Out There

"That is a great tie," Dean smiled and said as he entered the corner meeting room where I had parked myself.

"Thanks. It took me some time to find this one," I quipped. "How have you been?" It had been a little more than a month since I had met him.

"I don't know." Dean looked away. His voice sounded tentative.

"Why? What happened? I thought it was going great, the last time we met," I asked curiously.

"Yeah. I had also thought so. But it's difficult, you know? These guys don't understand the nuts and bolts of it. But they want to have a say in everything. And the budgets have been slashed. I have not gotten the approvals on the additional headcount. The Finance team thinks they rule the kingdom. They tell us the margins are not good enough. Why should I go to them to get these approvals? Have they ever seen the data that their pricing team sends? A sophomore can do better."

It was as if I had opened the floodgate of a dam. I listened to Dean patiently.

"I hear what you are saying. It seems that there are several hurdles in the way. Let's talk about how we can deal with them one-by-one," I suggested.

"So, what all options can you think of to address the budget situation?" I quizzed.

"I told Pali that we need to bring some subject-matter experts on board. But he did not listen to me. Now we are at the mercy of the client. Their COO did not even blink an eye, looking at our last presentation. And he goes gaga over our competition," Dean continued.

"Ok. What do you think can help you face the competition better?" I tried hard to have him focus on the issue at hand. But I failed.

"I don't know. Who can make them understand what it is to be in the trenches? We lost the deal. Our folks are not up to the level. The competition is killing us. Aventa has come up with this great proposition, and they already were playing on cost. It's just a matter of time. It's a jungle out there, I tell you."

Dean was touted as a rising star, someone who could scale up to become a successor to the head of business in the next 2 years. It was that very reason why Pali, who was the head of business that time, had urged me to coach Dean.

In Psychology, externalization is often referred to as situations wherein we project our internal traits to the external world. Simply put, it is the phenomenon where one may feel that things that are happening to him or her are because of external circumstances that are independent of him/her. It is argued that people do this subconsciously at times, as part of a defense mechanism to safeguard themselves from critique and blame. As you can see from the conversation, Dean was externalizing his situation. He sounded as if he were helpless and could not do anything to move ahead. This held him back from focusing on what he could do to move ahead. He had surrendered his power to his circumstances. We too, like Dean, externalize our problems and challenges, attributing them at times to others, to the circumstances, or to our destiny.

The Courtroom Drama

Primetime television has been abuzz with legal TV shows for years. Each episode grips the viewers, leaving them asking for more. They have the perfect recipe with inexplicable cases, blind turns of events, intimidating stories, sleuth lawyers, and intense arguments of proof. And all of it to bring forth the truth. One can feel the sheer intensity of the trial, even if it is on the television. The scene inside our minds is similar. Of the many functions that our subconscious mind performs, it also acts as a court. Deep inside its hollows, it presides over cases of happenings, to investigate the evidence and facts to arrive at the truth – why things happened the way they happened.

Our brain does not like gaps, and it works incessantly to fill them. This phenomenon is also the reason why we never have blind spots in our vision. Our brain fills in the missing pieces of information. It does so to create a likely picture, which we end up understanding as the truth. The same principle is applied in the event of a failure. The need to complete the picture requires the reasoning of why things did not work out. The mechanisms of the brain do this as part of our survival adaptation so that we don't make the same mistakes again. This mechanism has helped humans remain safe from external threats as part of our evolution process.

Inside the subconscious, the court convenes, and the trial begins. The available facts are presented and assessed to arrive at what happened and why. In the event of a lack of information about "why," the brain fills in the information. More likely than not, it is in line with what is in your Deep Script. Based on the assessment of the information, a verdict is passed, citing the reasons for failure. The reasons may be intrinsic (your ability, effort, perseverance, etc.) or extrinsic (opportunities, support from others, luck, fate, etc.). Often, we are unaware of these proceedings since these happen deep within, however, the effects of it can be realized if we remain aware.

Sometimes the nature of the verdict ends up reinforcing our Deep Script. Let's imagine that your Deep Script has it that luck does not favor you. The next time you witness a setback, there are high chances that the reasons for your fall will be attributed either completely or in part to your luck. This happens because your Deep Script fills in the missing pieces of the information required by your subconscious mind to arrive at the verdict. The verdict will rule your luck guilty. This instance further reinforces your Deep Script that your luck does not favor you. You can see how this works as a loop.

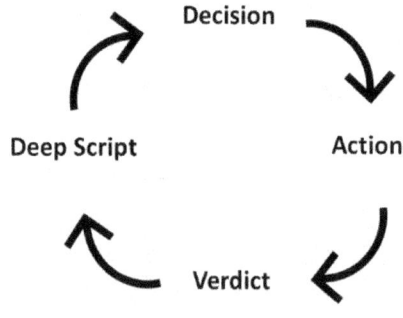

The Self-Fulfilling Loop

It is important to understand how this narrative impacts your subsequent decisions and actions. If you think that you will not succeed no matter how hard you work, you may choose not to take up certain projects or assignments. That may be an opportunity lost. More importantly, this feeling of not being supported enough may weigh you down over a period. Due to this, even the goals you could easily achieve may seem unsurmountable.

5. Why Setbacks Are Helpful

The Exile of Ambition

"What is that? It sounds like some strange bird, as if someone is forcing it to call? Is that sound coming from the woods?" Ashley quizzed our tour guide.

"It is the common Poorwill," he responded like an enlightened soul.

"Common what?" she asked with a smile, about to burst into laughter.

"Poorwill. I know, right," he said, joining the revelry.

What caught my attention about this bird was more than its name or the call. The common Poorwills are nocturnal birds found in parts of North America. What is unique about them is the fact that they are the only bird species that go into torpor, or extended hibernation, in winters. Most birds fly thousands of miles and migrate to other parts of the world when winters arrive. But the Poorwill goes into hiding under rocks for extended periods when the weather gets cold. Rather than braving the long, arduous flight, they tend to sleep it away in glory. The euphemism in their name *(poor-willed)* may be more than a coincidence. While nature may have built the poor bird that way, we humans do have a choice.

Like the Poorwill, a lot of people, too, when faced with setbacks put themselves in hibernation. They drop their arms and give up in the face of adversity. The chains of failure become so heavy that it becomes difficult for them to move. Philosophers, thinkers, and psychologists have recognized this unique trait of not giving up in many forms. Whether you call it willpower, determination, persistence, perseverance, or grit, it is key for success.

We all have an innate desire to be fit and remain healthy. But according to the recent statistics published by *The Hustle* on gym memberships and usage, 63% of memberships go completely unused, and 82% of gym members go to the gym less than once per week. Moreover, 22% completely stop going six months into their membership, and 31% say they never would have paid had they known how little they would use it. According to a 2018 *Finder.com* survey, Americans spent an estimated $1.8 billion on gym memberships but never used them. Like these, there are many indicators of our persistence.

Similarly, when faced with setbacks, a lot of people give up, never to return to their pursuits. We need to reflect upon our response to adversity. Do we give up and lock away our desires in hibernation, or do we get back at it? Grace Murray Hopper once said, "A ship in harbor is safe, but that is not what ships are built for." Remembering that setbacks are temporary is key. You can overcome your lack of will by making the desire very intense. The setbacks are not the real failures. Failure is when you give up on your desires.

Of Strong Winds and Heavy Rains

"But, why do I have to study more? It's six o'clock and my friends would have come to play by now," my little niece protested.

"Because the tests start on Monday, and you need to review the syllabus before that," my mother retorted.

"Please let me go, Aaji," she pleaded to her grandmother, making a puppy face.

"Ok. But you have to promise that you will complete the pending parts tomorrow," It seemed like they had struck a deal. The next day, my mother, as persistent as she was, took the book and placed it in the hands of my little niece. The expressions on her face said it all. The pact had to be honored.

My niece reluctantly flipped the pages of the book. Her keenness to study was evident with the grumbling which followed, "Why do we have to take tests? They are difficult."

The innocent expression made my mother smile. "Let me tell you a story," she said. I, enjoying a cup of tea, quietly observed the duo as they set off on an adventure.

Once there was a farmer who used to toil hard every day in his field. He used to start from his house early in the morning, to return only at dark. Sun or rain, he would keep at it. One day, as he woke up from his bed, he looked outside the window. What he saw woke him up completely. The sky was overcast. "This is not the time of the year," he mumbled. As he was about to leave the house, it started pouring. The farmer sat in his house feeling frustrated. He grew worried about the crop. The day passed by and night fell, but the thoughts played repeatedly in his head. That night, the farmer had a dream. In his dream, he stood in front of God. He argued, "Why do you do this? I work hard night and day." The anguish in his voice was apparent. "You send rain and thunderstorms. Why?" he demanded.

"Because that is how nature works," God replied with a smile.

"You have created nature. And let me tell you if that is how it works, it is flawed," said the farmer without mincing his words.

"Ok, I hear you. So, how would you like it?" God asked the farmer curiously.

"Let me decide," the farmer proposed.

"Ok," God replied with a smile.

The next morning, the farmer, still confused by the dream, tried to test his hand. He stood in the center of his field looking up and waved his hands. A strong gust of wind started blowing. He could not believe it. He then pointed at the sky. The clouds followed the command and gathered over the field. He held his hand out, and it began to rain. The farmer was elated. He had the power now.

Armed with his new abilities, the farmer continued to work in his field. He would summon the weather whenever he wanted and kept the clouds and wind at bay. The field was lush with the crop.
One bright morning, the farmer sprang out of bed. He could not hold in his excitement as he walked towards his field. It was time to harvest.

His excitement did not last long. As he started from one side of the field, he exclaimed, "How could this be?"

He waded through to the other side of the field to check. "This is impossible." The farmer kept checking the crop for hours. He finally returned home in despair. That night, he again met God in his dream. "What did you do?" he demanded.

"I did nothing, my son," God replied.

"I worked hard and looked after my field. I managed the weather well. I kept the winds and rain away. Then how did the grains disappear from my crop?" the farmer asked. "I am sure you did something to sabotage my crop," he continued.

"My dear son, I did nothing. I gave you the power," God said with a kind smile.

"Then, how did this happen?" The farmer looked puzzled.

"When strong winds blew and rain poured, it forced the roots of the crop to go deeper to hold themselves in good stead. As the roots went deeper, they got more nourishment from the soil and the grain got bigger. You kept the winds and rain away," God explained.

The farmer, having realized his mistake, apologized profusely to God and requested that his power be taken back. "I understand, my Lord," he said as he woke up.

My niece had now picked up her book, smiling.

We face many adversities in the pursuit of our desires. Strong headwinds make it difficult to move ahead. Heavy rains dampen our spirit. But what if there were no adversities? You could get what you want with just a wave of your hand, just like the farmer summoning the Sun and the rain. Wouldn't it be great? No.

The lack of adversity can lead to some significant issues:

- A sense of entitlement may set in since you don't need to strive for an outcome. This can be damaging in the long run, as one may expect results on their own without putting in enough effort.
- The focus to build our capabilities for the present and, more importantly, for the future may be missing. When individuals don't anticipate the needs of the future, they miss the opportunity to invest in themselves.

- After a difficult situation or a challenge, we are less likely to be impacted as much the next time we face something of similar magnitude. This is usually understood as resilience. It builds our threshold for pain.

However, it is easier said than done, one may argue. When faced with a challenge, it is difficult to remember all this. And hence, we need to ask ourselves, How do we usually react when we are faced with adversity? Do our responses and thoughts sound like "Oh no, not again," "Why me," "Why now?"

Adversities challenge our thinking faculties and force us to explore our paradigms. The challenges help us expand our horizons and step beyond what we think we know. Sometimes we may know the significance of the wind and rain for the crops, and sometimes we may not. But reminding yourself that you will only come out stronger and more resilient will help you face the storm.

The Tutelage of Saturn

My father, who was a Professor of Physics, had developed a keen interest in the subject of Astronomy and as an extension to that, in Astrology, from his college days. I have distinct memories of when I was about five years old, flipping through pages of the Astronomy magazine, feeling fascinated looking at the images of the galaxies and stars. A distinct memory of mine from that time was that of one special evening. I still remember rushing to the terrace, running after my father. He had been talking about some apparatus and had promised to bring it home one day from his lab. The excitement was too hard to contain. As my father unpacked and assembled that thing, I felt as if some magic was about to unfold. My elder brother and I jostled to have a look. It was a telescope. We saw the crevices of the moon and its dark side. I will never forget the awe that evening had instilled in my young mind. After taking us to the moon and back, our father continued to look through the expanse of the night sky as if he were looking for something. I quietly sat on the ledge, looking at him and then looking at the sky, letting the feeling sink in. I asked him, "What are you looking for, Papa?" as he fixed his gaze in a direction. "Come here, I will show you," he said with a smile. A yellow dot appeared in the lens as I wondered what it was. I was a bit disappointed to look at this, after seeing the magnificence of the moon. "This is Saturn, the great teacher," he said.

Saturn is the sixth planet from the Sun in our solar system. With its illustrious rings, it is one of the most prominent planets. It has been a subject of curiosity amongst astronomers, mythologists, astrologers, psychologists, and thinkers alike since prehistoric times. Due to this, Saturn has been depicted in various ways. In mythology and astrology, it is believed that Saturn is a teacher and a taskmaster. It is also believed that Lord Saturn guards the Gates of Initiation, putting you to test to check if you are ready to move through it. The learning that he offers is often associated with patience, sacrifice, hard work, and attention to detail. His teaching is often considered to be difficult, as he ensures that we confront the reality, scrutinize the details, and learn the lessons diligently.

It was late in the afternoon, and the look on Aaron's face depicted a concoction of thoughts and feelings – he was amazed that I said it, he was curious why I said it, he was wondering where I was going with it, and at the same time he was annoyed that I meant it when I said it.

"Really?" The frustration in his voice was evident.

I nodded. And smiled, to add some fuel to the fire.

I had started to enjoy this conversation and, honestly, the annoyance of Aaron, too. I could see him turn red and the valley between his eyebrows deepening.

"Are you telling me that this was good? Are you out of your mind? On what earth can this be good?" The temperature of the conversation just went up by a couple of degrees. He went on, "I don't understand why this had to happen now. It is like lord Saturn has his eyes on me."

Aaron and I had just stepped out of a meeting with his client. To cool off before we boarded our plane, we had parked ourselves at a beer lounge at the airport. Back in the days when I used to work for a large consulting firm, we used to sometimes go along with our peers to accompany them to client meetings. This was our way of keeping abreast of industry trends. That day, I had accompanied Aaron. The agenda of the day-long client meeting was to present the preliminary findings, take stock of the project status, and share some updates and discussions with the key stakeholders on the way forward. Everything had gone better than expected. But there was one problem.

In the middle of the presentation, we sensed that there was some confusion regarding the committed timelines of the project. The client team's perception of the duration was significantly lesser than what we had committed to. And this was unearthed in the meeting that day. Aaron and I could quickly sense that something was not right, but that was not the time to highlight it as all key client stakeholders were present in the room. It would have been a source of major embarrassment for Julie, who was the Head of Customer Success, and our key client counterpart. We kept quiet then and spoke to Julie in our discussion later in the day. We realized that the project team had made an error when putting the estimated timelines in the proposal. They had accidentally mentioned 23 weeks instead of the actual estimate of 32 weeks. A small typo, that's all it was. But the discrepancy of 9 weeks meant that Aaron and the team had less time to deliver. Even the thought of it was giving Aaron jitters. Julie did not budge. She was adamant that we should have checked and that we will need to deliver within 23 weeks, as the timeline was already committed to her management team. It was not looking good.

Now, let us get back to the conversation with Aaron. I suggested to him that it was good that it happened. As much I was enjoying needling Aaron, I meant every word of what I said.

I clarified, "It is good that we are getting to know of this now, rather than a couple of weeks later. Then we would have no chance to do anything about it. Now that Julie also knows about the error, the feasibility of 23 weeks will be on her mind too. I am sure between you and Julie, you can find a way out. And lastly, if you have to aim for 23 weeks, you will get to know what the best-case scenario for such assignments is. It will be good learning for all subsequent projects."

Aaron heard me out and nodded, "Yea, I guess." And I can assure you it was not the beer talking.

This is not an uncommon scenario. Breakdowns happen. Setbacks are a part of our lives.

"It will get better, don't worry," my mother consoled my 2-year-old niece. "You need to look while walking," she said while wiping away my niece's tears and massaging her knee. My niece had stumbled and fallen in the excitement of chasing a kitten. When we are young, physical pain teaches us what to pay attention to and when to be careful. The learning we draw from our initial years helps us remain safe throughout our lives. Similarly, the existence of psychological or emotional pain indicates that something in our system is out of order. The pain of rejection or failure impresses upon us to avoid making the same mistakes in the future. Sometimes, a temporary setback also unearths a profound insight that may have been overlooked previously.

Spencer Silver had spent considerable time trying to come up with a strong adhesive formula. It was the area of focus at 3M, and Silver was entrusted with this venture. After weeks and months of prototyping and testing, the result was nowhere close to what he had wanted. What he had come up with was the exact opposite of what was wanted – an adhesive that could come off easily. His instinctual reaction was, "Who would want a glue that does not stick hard?" But after some time, Silver went back to his lab and realized there could be a potential use. Along with another colleague Art Fry, Silver started applying the adhesive to paper bookmarks. Thus, the post-it notes were born. If Silver had not looked beyond his setback, the world would have never had his product.

Adversity and setbacks are teachers. They teach us the hard way. But, if we can keep ourselves from drowning in the pain and look above the surface, often the insight appears. To complete the story, Aaron and the team managed to deliver the project in 26 weeks. That is 3 weeks over the committed date but 6 weeks below the estimate. It was a lesson learned not just in terms of avoiding mistakes but in terms of optimizing efforts and that the project could be delivered efficiently. It was a win-win for the client as well as for us.

6. Addressing the Fear of Failure

The Tale of Two Cousins

Many moons ago, there was a small village inhabited by simple folks. Kind and humble, the villagers used to lead a quiet and peaceful life. One day, a strange murmur enveloped the whole village. It was about some visitors. Everyone was curious to know more. The news had spread that the village had witnessed the arrival of two cousins. In line with the tradition, the villagers invited the two cousins for supper. But strange things started to happen with the hosts after the two cousins visited. No one knew why it was happening. Rumor had it that the two cousins had strange magical powers. The villagers who had witnessed them described the two cousins, Do and Fe, to the rest.

Do was small and beguiling. He could easily sneak through the doors and small openings. It was difficult to notice his innocuous presence and he would always appear to be on the side of the host. The other cousin, Fe, was big and made his presence felt. He would overwhelm others by his size. Fe used to threaten the hosts and feast on the host's food. He would make them do what he wanted them to. This was not all. Do used to sneak into houses where they were invited earlier and call Fe in to feast. Once they entered a house, it was difficult to get them to leave. Nobody knew how or from where they came. But one thing was certain. When one was present, the other one was sure to follow.

The villagers grew tired of the two cousins. They started to maintain vigil and kept checking with each other to see if anyone had seen the two cousins. Now and then, they would search their houses thoroughly to check if Do and Fe were hiding anywhere.

Have you ever witnessed the presence of the two cousins? I am sure you have. Let me share their full names, and you might recollect. Do is Doubt and Fe is Fear. We all have met them at various junctures in our lives. Armed with their names now, I invite you to read the story again. Imagine that you were the host in the story and your mind was the house.

Fear and Doubt are not new for us. We witness them periodically in our lives. What is important, though, is what you do when you meet them. Do you invite them for supper and let them stay, or do you keep your houses clean to get them going? It is important to remember that in the journey of success, we will keep meeting Do and Fe multiple times. If you let them stay, they will happily make your house theirs. But if you become aware of their presence and clean your house, their visits will be short and sweet. They will not bother you.

A Matter of Choice

I admire people who can bake well. This is because of two reasons: first, I love cakes, and second, I don't know how to bake them. I recollect the horror of trying to bake a cake once after watching a video on *YouTube*. The chef made it look so simple that it was enough to motivate me to put on the apron. The Saturday trip to the store ensured all ingredients were handy. My date with the oven was set for Sunday afternoon. My enthusiasm was on point. The ingredients were measured accurately. The mixing was done diligently. The timer was set perfectly. The moment of truth arrived as the timer of the oven went off. But the culinary Gods were in a different mood that day. As soon as I took the cake out, it wobbled like jelly and then crumbled in front of my eyes. I just could not take it. A whole week had been spent in anticipation, followed by hours of preparation. To this day, I try and hide my disappointment by joking about my baking abilities. A few weeks back, my dear sister-in-law and I were chatting about the cake that she had baked, when she suggested that it was very easy and I could do it, too. It brought back the memories of my baking encounter. How could I forget it?

Failure has been described in many ways by psychologists and theologists, as well as scientists. I see it as a perspective of actions and results. You take an action that produces a certain result. Often, there is an inherent expectation in terms of how this result should be. When we meet or exceed the expectations, we qualify the endeavor as a success. When we do not meet the expectations, we label it as a failure. The actions that you take and the result that your actions cause are facts. The meanings that we then further attach to the results are just labels. Going back to my baking encounter, my act of baking and the resultant crumbly cake are facts. It is also a fact that the cake did not come up even close to my expectations. Disappointed by the debacle, I can tell myself that I am terrible at baking. It can go further, and I can pronounce that I am no good in the kitchen. All of these are labels that I am attaching to the result.

The perspective of failure is a perspective of choice. You always have the choice of either looking at the facts or adding a label to them. It is important to note the consequences of this choice. If I choose to limit myself to the facts, my narrative would look like, "I tried to bake a cake. It did not turn out per my expectations." The implication is that I would not beat myself up forever for missing on the cake. I might regain my confidence to try it out again someday. It leaves the door open. However, if I choose to affix a label to it, my narrative would look like, "I tried to bake a cake. It did not turn out per my expectations. I am horrible at baking. I am no good in the kitchen." What do you think will be my response the next time someone invites me to try again? I would have left no room to go back to it again.

At times, when faced with failures and setbacks, we get stuck in a downward spiral. We add multiple layers of meanings and labels to the facts at hand. The facts are swept aside, and the problem is exaggerated so much that we make a choice – to pronounce ourselves defeated.

Failure is not when you do not get the desired results. Failure is when you decide that you have failed and give up.

So how can one know when she or he is stuck in the downward spiral?

The ancient Hindu scripture, the *Rig Veda*, mentions Hamsa, a mystical Swan that can separate milk from water, when the two are mixed. Lord Brahma, the God of creation and the creator of the universe, rides the Hamsa. One of the mantras, the Hamsa Gayatri mantra, is dedicated to the unique ability of the Hamsa:

Om Hamsaaya Vidmahe
Paramahamsaaya Dhimahi
Tanno Hamsa Prachodayaat

"May we realize Hamsa that is our Self. Let us meditate on that Paramahamsa, the Supreme Self. May Hamsa illumine us."

To distinguish if we are contemplating the truth or if we are stuck in the spiral, we must incite the Hamsa-like ability in ourselves to discern the truth from the meaning. We need to distinguish the facts from the labels that we are attaching.

Points for Reflection

Step 1: Identify any of your recent significant setbacks.

Step 2: Write down the answers to the following questions, in the context of the setback:
- What do I know about the situation at hand?
- What are the facts?
- How do I know that it is a fact?
- What is left of what I know?
- What meaning and labels am I attaching?

Step 3: Segregate the facts from the meaning.

Step 4: Reflect upon how the meaning and labels have impacted your subsequent thoughts and actions.

The Fear of Failure

Lot of people wonder how to overcome our fear. We have all heard the phrase "Survival of the fittest." It depicts the key narrative of the evolutionary history of species and highlights the presence of basic survival instincts. In the initial phases of evolution, humans lived in the wilderness. To ensure protection from predators and other dangers, the human brain evolved adaptive responses. These responses were triggered by the brain in the event of perceived danger. The three responses were fight (offensive), flight (retreat), and freeze (no action). Each of these responses included physiological reactions. Most of the time, the reactions were not conscious decisions. They were automatic and guided by the brain. While we as humans have evolved and do not face predatory dangers now, interestingly our reactions to perceived fear have not evolved.

When faced with the fear of failure, we respond in similar ways. We either choose flight, by not facing the challenge and giving up, or we freeze and go into hibernation. Sometimes, we choose to fight and move ahead to act. The effect of the flight and freeze reactions is plagued by a lack of persistence and not in the favor of achievement.

However, the fear of failure has some positive aspects, too. It helps us question our preparedness. If done right, this can help significantly in robust planning of efforts as well as planning for contingencies. The fear can also, when channeled in the right direction, fuel persistence and ensure continuity of effort. It can make you invest in your abilities and keep you from taking shortcuts.

The key is to pivot the fear of failure to your advantage, shifting the focus from a flight or freeze reaction to fueling your planning and persistence.

The Fuel to The Fire

There can be several causes of a fear of failure. These can range from intrinsic factors such as issues in dealing with ambiguity or lack of self-belief, to acquired or external factors such as recent events or mishaps. However, I have noticed some key causes are more prevalent in people whom I have worked with as a coach:

- Constant Comparisons with Others – The tendency to benchmark one's life with others is common in many of us. By the same virtue, we also end up measuring how good our successes are and how bad our failures are. We tend to forget that the context of no two individuals is the same. By the same logic, no two successes or failures can be of the same magnitude.

- Worry About Perceptions – "What would my family think of me?" "Would my friends and colleagues laugh at me?" "Will people call me a loser?" Many such thoughts haunt us when we think and allow the perception of others to define who we are and what we are capable of. While the thoughts and feelings of our loved ones may be important for us to consider, it is important to remind ourselves of this fact – "My goals are my goals. They are not of my neighbors, not of my friends and colleagues, and may not even be of my family."

- Lack of Belief – Peter McIntyre once said very aptly, "Confidence comes not from always being right but from not fearing to be wrong." When faced with a challenge, people tend to doubt their abilities. Questions such as "Am I good enough?" "Will I be able to do this?" "What if I fail?" start clouding our thoughts. The lack of belief can quickly turn into a flight or a freeze response. I have personally found a lot of merit in the advice given by Vincent Van Gogh, one of the most celebrated painters and pioneers of modern art. He said, "If you hear a voice within you say, 'you cannot paint,' then by all means paint, and that voice will be silenced."

- Dealings With Past Failures – Past failures can impede the efforts of the present, especially when the desires of the past were of intense magnitude. We will explore this fear in detail in the next chapter.

Clearing the Fog

Fear is one of the most primitive yet powerful emotions that we have experienced as humans. Fear alerts us to the presence of any danger and stimulates our defense mechanism. Fear has a wide range in terms of its intensity, ranging from mild trepidation to the other extreme of intense horror. While people often correctly realize the presence of this powerful emotion through physiological and cognitive reactions, they at times find it difficult to cope with. There are many ways of addressing fear. In this section, we will look at some techniques, which have proven to help address the fear of failure:

- Dissociation – When you step out of the boxing ring in an imaginative bout with fear, it empowers you to look at the situation from a 360-degree perspective. Just as sunlight clears the fog, clarity clears fear. Being clear about the various nuances of the situation can help you revisit thoughts and perspectives not only about the situation, but fear itself. A temporary dissociation from the situation can significantly help achieve that.

- Isolation – Often people feel overwhelmed due to the fear of failure. In a short period, the fear of failure can look like a big mountain, difficult to overcome. Breaking the issue down into smaller pieces can help make the situation more manageable. We need to remember that the whole situation may not be an issue. A part of it is creating fear. When you chunk the situation down, it helps isolate the exact issue from the larger situation.

- Looking for the "Yes" – Every "No" has a "Yes" hidden in it. Every adversity brings forth an opportunity along with it. The inability to pull heavy loads with horse carriages led to the invention of cars. The Y2K crisis led to the rise of the Information Technology industry. Reminding yourself that there is a hidden opportunity can allay the intensity of the fear.

- The "Not Yet" mindset – When you replace a "No" with a "Not Yet" in your answer to the questions and thoughts around whether you have succeeded, it can bring in a radical change in paradigm. A "No" is absolute and binary. "Not Yet" signifies that the process is not over yet. You can work further to improve the results. It empowers you since now you have the choice.

- Plan B – Unlike movies, most situations in our lives are not stark "prevail or perish" situations. There is always a possible third result. Thinking about your possible actions in case of a failure can help alleviate the fear of failure. Having a Plan B can help you overcome the otherwise overwhelming result and move forward.

Part III - Getting Unstuck

"Be not the slave of your own past - plunge into the sublime seas, dive deep, and swim far, so you shall come back with new self-respect, with new power, and with an advanced experience that shall explain and overlook the old."

— Ralph Waldo Emerson

7. Letting Your Past Be Your Past

The Trails of Smoke

The windows started rattling. The sound was very loud and distinct from anything I had ever heard. Curious, I rushed to the deck to catch a glimpse. As I looked up, I saw a magnificent F-16 Thunderbird fighter jet flying above. It seemed so distant above in the sky, though the roar of the engines was almost deafening. The two wings left a long, magnificent trail of smoke behind as the jet disappeared in the clouds. The smoke trail remained visible for a long time, as a testament to the path of the jet.

I wondered what made the jet fly so high. The combustion of the fuel in the powerful engines propels the jet forward. While one may see smoke behind the jet, it is not the smoke that makes the jet move forward. The smoke is just a residue. Our life is also like this jet. It moves ahead, leaving a trail of our past. But it is not our past which moves us forward. Often, I hear people blaming the challenges and the hardships of their past for their present conditions. The failures we have witnessed in the past continue to dictate our decisions of the present. We continue to relive the past again and again.

We revisit our trails for two distinct reasons:

1. Lack of Completeness with the Past – A lot of times, residual feelings of despair, guilt, and anger remain with us for a long period, after the event. This usually is the case when we are not able to get over the results or the reasons for it. We beat ourselves up for reasons of failure that we attribute to ourselves, e.g. "I wish I had worked harder," "I could have asked for help from person X." In other cases, we blame fate and others for the lack of results. In short, we have not made peace with the failure. We feel helpless in breaking the chains of the past that tie us down.

2. Ambiguity of the Future – The human brain is built to bring predictability in situations. It is its natural modus operandi, a part of the human survival instinct. Let's look at the scenario of driving to work every day. We end up taking a specific route most of the days. Because it is familiar, we don't need to keep looking at where we need to make turns or constantly check if we are in the right direction. Imagine taking a new route every day. It would be exhausting. We see the future as somewhat unpredictable, and our brain falls back on what we know and what is familiar: our past.

While exploring our past can help us draw insights and prepare ourselves better, delving too much into it does not help. Constantly reliving the memories of the past can lead to a detachment from the present. One may tend to lose focus. Moments of life may just pass by without us realizing it. When we get too attached to the past, we also tend to lose sight of the future. We may not invest in preparing ourselves adequately. Replaying the failures of the past brings negative thoughts, which in turn generate negative emotions. Experiencing such emotions over a considerable period can lead to physical, emotional, as well as mental ailments. Lack of sleep, anxiety, depression, bouts of anger, and lack of enthusiasm are just some of them.

The Default Future

Thoughts lead to emotions. When we think of something, it creates a bio-chemical reaction inside our brain. This reaction leads to the secretion of certain hormones. This corresponds to physical sensations in the body, which is how we experience emotions. Let's look at an example. You are walking towards your new car, ready to drive to work. Just as you are a few meters away from the car, you see a man intentionally scratching your car with his key. Looking at the big scratch on your new car, you get angry and approach the man. In this case, you would observe your heart rate and blood pressure increase. Your body temperature would rise, leading to perspiration. In a way, your brain sends signals, based on your thoughts, to the rest of the body to instruct it on how to feel. While the thoughts are created and interpreted in the brain, the feelings are manifested in the body.

When you think about failures and setbacks of the past, you send continuous signals to your body to experience negative emotions. The constant playback of such thoughts establishes the pattern in your brain. Over a period, this establishes a habit. Every time your brain senses a pause in thoughts, it goes back to its habitual pattern and plays the thoughts of the past. It then instructs your body, and you start reliving the feeling again. This pattern has also been described by many as an "autopilot" behavior.

When your brain continues to think of past failures, your body experiences disempowering emotions. This transfers into your decisions and actions. When your thoughts, feelings, and actions all align to the past, your results also follow suit. We recreate our past failures, and this goes on as a loop. While it may look very stark, this helps us understand the importance of our thoughts and emotions in the process of manifesting the results.

The Recourse of The Fallen

Repeated failures can create disillusionment within us. After having worked hard, the lack of expected results leads to significant disappointment. People often see giving up as the only resort, understandably so. It seems to be the obvious choice when nothing seems to work. This often is amplified when people have faced other setbacks in their past. They start drawing correlations between the past and the present, arriving at conclusions for their future, such as "This is not meant for me" or "I am just wasting my time on this." They drop their arms tired and defeated, never to pick them up again.

Katheryn was born in 1984 in Santa Barbara, California, to her pastor parents. She grew up in a conservative family. Both of her parents were pastors, and they refused to let her listen to any rock or popular music. But her heart was into music. She started taking singing lessons to pursue a career aligned with her passion. Katheryn got her first break with a label to record a gospel album. Invigorated by the opportunity, Katheryn stayed the course. But the album did not do well, and in a couple of months, the label went bankrupt. Katheryn moved on without the setback dampening her spirit. She moved to Los Angeles to find work. She signed on with a producer who had worked with other significant artists. But it did not bear results. Katheryn struggled for years being on her own with no money. She sold her clothes to pay rent and borrowed money from others to live on. It was becoming more and more difficult. Katheryn and her producer approached many record companies, but no one was willing to take them on board. In 2003, she signed with Island Def Jam, however, the contract was terminated.

In 2004 she got an opportunity to collaborate with music producers, The Matrix. Katheryn saw a ray of hope. The string of disappointments continued for Katheryn, though. Unfortunately, the record was scrapped before it was about to release. She had witnessed three major setbacks in her career. Having worked very hard for it, it seemed like a never-ending struggle.

Giving up would have seemed like the obvious choice to Katheryn, but she didn't. She continued to pursue her career, working odd jobs and doing back-up vocals. She persisted. And then, her break came. She was signed up by a new company, Capitol Music Group, in 2006. Her first single, "I Kissed a Girl," went on to become a huge hit. She continued to strive further. She won a Grammy nomination for her first single. Her subsequent tracks went on to top the Billboard charts. She became only the second artist, after Michael Jackson, to have five No.

1 hits from a single album. With many hits under her name, Katheryn went on to become one of the most successful pop artists of our time: Katy Perry.

Our road to achieving maximum results may be full of hurdles. The setback may be a part of the journey. While giving up is always an option, it is important to remember that it is not the only option you have. Get up, again!

Time Travelling

Moving through different points of time has been a subject of keen interest of many for decades. Many science fiction movies and TV shows have depicted this ability more like a superpower. There are many theories on whether time travel is possible or not, and the perspectives continue to evolve with more research in the area. In his seminal work, "The Theory of Relativity," Einstein proposed that time was a sort of an illusion. It was relative and varied for observers depending on their speed through space. Time also provided another coordinate of space: the direction.

If you visualize these elements, anything that is behind you is the past. Anything that is in front of you is the future. Where you are in this moment is the present. By default, you move ahead towards the future, and the space that you cover keeps becoming your past. As you are moving in a direction, time passes you in the other direction. It is like swimming in a river of time where the current is against you. The stronger the current, the more effort is required to move ahead. The strong current also at times takes you back in your past.

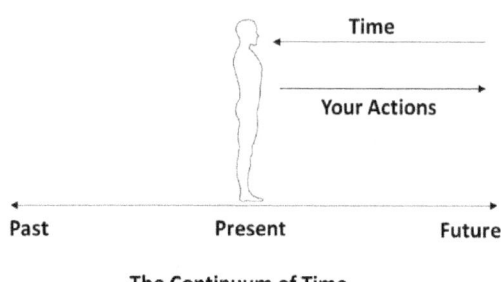

The Continuum of Time

While physical time travel has not yet been made possible, we have all traveled through the three realms of time cognitively. Our conscious awareness of the moment ensures that we are in the realm of the present. When we think of our dreams, desires, and goals, they take us on a flight to the realm of the future. We visualize how it will be once we have achieved them. At that moment, we are living in a possible glimpse of the future. When we think of our memories and remember events that have happened months or years ago, we are reliving our past. We do many such trips and travel across this continuum of past, present, and future multiple times a day. Most of the time, we do not even realize it. We end up covering lightyears' worth of time distance while traveling across these three realms.

The realm of the future houses the outcomes, the realm of the past houses the memories, and the realm of the present houses the choices. Your outcomes of the future are always dependent on the choices you make in the present. When you don't make conscious choices from the present, the stream of time washes you away to the shores of the past. Your choices, then, reflect what you could or could not achieve in your past. Mother Teresa very aptly said, "Yesterday is gone. Tomorrow has not yet come. We have only today. Let us begin."

There are many ways in which you can ensure that you always create from the present. Meditation and centering exercises can help you become aware and be in the present more often. Here are some ways that can help you in your journey:

- The Gift of Forgiveness – Sometimes we let the chains of our past failures tie us down in our present. Feelings of guilt, shame, anger, and despair loom over our decisions and actions. When we are incomplete with our past, we are not able to move forward. Forgiving ourselves and others for the actions and results of yesterday is the only way to move on. When you forgive yourself for the past and present, you give yourself a second chance for the future. Lewis Smedes once said, "To forgive is to set a prisoner free and discover that the prisoner was you."

- The Secret Torch – A lot of times, we find it difficult to get over the challenges that we are faced with. The dark fog clouds our ability to think. A secret torch can help dispel this darkness. This secret torch is "Now What?" For example, John was struggling with the losses in his business. His company had gone bankrupt, and it seemed like everything was over. He was not able to find the strength to get up. He then turned the secret torch on and asked himself, "I have lost my business. Now what?" The question made him think hard, and two options emerged. He could go back to his job or try again. The power of "Now What" immediately helped him make peace with what had happened and cleared the way forward by bringing the choice back to him. He found himself back in the driver's seat.

- The Inner Compass – Earlier in this chapter, we explored how emotions are manifested due to our thoughts. We also realized that when we are not consciously thinking, the cross-currents of time wash us back. The thoughts from our past come to the forefront. These thoughts then generate residual emotions. One way to realize if we are being washed out by the currents is to notice our emotional state. Our emotions act like buoys in the sea, helping us navigate the currents. When you realize your emotional state, you can always trace it back to the thoughts that are creating it.

- The Occasional Brake – You apply brakes in a moving vehicle when you either want to stop or slow down. Applying the brake to your thoughts by asking "What's happening?" is similar to that. Like the X-Ray scanner at the airport projects the content of a bag on the screen, the question "What's happening?" projects your baggage of thoughts running in your head at that moment. Applying the brake occasionally helps you realize your thoughts and brings you back to the present moment.

8. Moving Beyond our Reasons

Stuck in the Web of "Too"

"Why not?" I quizzed. She looked at me and smiled sheepishly. "Didn't you always want to do that?"

"Yes, but that was then," she quipped while getting up from the dinner table as if she was trying to get away from my probing.

"So, what has changed?" I persisted.

"Who would want to get their logos and campaigns designed by an old lady," she laughed in self-deprecating humor. "And besides, everything has changed - the software, the new tools. I don't know any of it. And I am too old to learn all that now."

This dear friend of mine is a mother of two. She was doing very well at an advertising agency when she decided to get married. Sally and her husband subsequently decided to start their family. She took a break from her corporate career to give their kids the upbringing that she wanted. And I must say, she did a fabulous job of it as a dedicated mother. The children had grown, and it was about time for them to pursue college and be on their own. The elder boy was to leave next Fall and the younger girl, in the subsequent year. Sally was already feeling the effects of empty nest syndrome. When she shared this with me over dinner, I remembered how she wanted to start her design venture. But as you can see, she was entangled in the web of being "too old" to pursue her dreams.

Too old or too young.

Too skinny or too overweight.

Too stable or too much in flux.

Too busy or too idle.

Too overwhelmed or too unaffected.

Too late or too soon.

And many more….

Our lives have too many of these reasons. See! There was a "too" in the last sentence as well.
We give reasons for why we should not act. And slowly, the *"should not"* takes the form of *"cannot."* While it may sound like wordplay, repetitively telling yourself something is a way of forming a pattern. And after a point, the pattern seems so overwhelming and large that one seems to be in a dark hollow, coming out of which becomes too

daunting. These reasons that we create and protect over the years hold our ambitions and dreams hostage.

One may wonder, where do these self-imposed reasons come from? Societal norms, our perceptions of ourselves, our perception of what others think of us, and many other factors contribute to these reasons. Our world view is defined by what is the "norm" in society. We accept these norms without even thinking about their relevance for us and our lives, even for a moment. This perspective is not meant to invite you to rebel against all societal norms. These norms help maintain order amongst chaos and establish ways of existing. They form the core foundation of societies, where people can harmoniously co-exist. However, at times we assume what the norms are, we assume how they apply to us and we assume how we should act, given the norms, as well.

If we go back to the example of Sally, she arrived at her conclusion through what we know as Inductive Reasoning. It is where one's experiences and observations, including things learned from others, are synthesized to come up with a conclusion. This is how her reasoning worked:

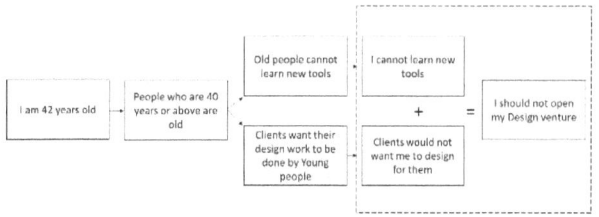

Inductive Reasoning Flow

We need to consider that this conclusion may or may not be true. And who gets to decide if it is true or not? The conversation with my friend made me think about what age has to do with achieving what you want. They say age is just a number. What matters most is how you let that number affect your thoughts and actions.

J.R.R Tolkien was 62 when *The Lord of the Rings* books came out. Ronald Reagan was 69 when he became President of the United States. Nelson Mandela was 76 when he became President of South Africa. These great men could have hung up their boots thinking they were too old to fulfill their dreams. Mozart was competent on the keyboard and violin and started composing from the age of 5. Helen Keller, at the age of 19 months, became deaf and blind. But that did not stop her. She was the first deaf and blind person to earn a Bachelor of Arts degree. If Mozart and Helen Keller had thought that they were too young, they would have never achieved the heights they did. The age of a person is a fact, but whether he or she is too young or too old is just a perception.

We have many such reasons operating in our lives in the background. We make decisions and take action in light of these reasons. It is important to evaluate if your reasons are helping you or acting as a hindrance to you living a fulfilling life. No matter what your reasons are – age, ability, experience, or anything else - ask yourself, "Are my reasons working for me or working against me?"

Point for Reflection

Here is a simple exercise that can help you deduce your reasons which are stopping you from taking action. You may need to dig deep for some of the reasons, as they may be deeply ingrained in you. This may require you to repeat this exercise multiple times, until you can reach the bottom of it.

Step 1: List the thoughts that you have about yourself, in the context of achieving your desires. (e.g. I am too old for that, I don't have the necessary know-how, etc.). Write down as many as you can think of.

I am _____

I am not_____

I have_____

I don't have _____

I can_____

I cannot_____

I should_____

I shouldn't_____

Step 2: For each of the thoughts that you have listed, ask yourself "Why do I feel that?" Write the answer for each of the thoughts.

E.g.

Thought	Why do I feel that?
I am too old for that	I am 42 years old
I cannot spend so much time on my business	My husband would not like that I take time away from family

Step 3: Reflect upon the answers. Ask yourself "How do I know?" This will help you separate the fact from the perception.

E.g.

Thought	Why do I feel that?	How do I know?
I am too old for that	I am 42 years old	My age is 42 years (fact) 42 years is too old (perception)
I cannot spend so much time on my business	My husband would not like that I take time away from family	Working on my business will require me to take time away from family (fact) My husband would not like that (this can be a fact or a perception and hence needs to be checked)

Step 4: Think about "What can I do to ascertain this perception?"

E.g.

Thought	Why do I feel that?	How do I know?	What can I do to ascertain this perception?
I am too old for that	I am 42 years old	My age is 42 years (fact) 42 years is too old (perception)	It is my perception, so I don't need to check with anyone else about it
I cannot spend so much time on my business	My husband would not like that I take time away from family	Working on my business will require me to take time away from family (fact) My husband would not like that (this can be a fact or a perception and hence needs to be checked)	I can speak to my husband about it to find out what he thinks

Who has The Power?

Do you let life happen to you, or are you making life happen? This question is at the core of our belief system. You need to ask yourself "Who is in control of your life?" "Who is in control of your results.?"

The truth is *you* are responsible for your success. Now, this may sound like a burden, right? You may also think, "I have heard this before, but it does not change anything." The key lies in our perspective towards it. As human beings, we are responsible for our own lives. Our behavior is a function of our decisions. We have the initiative and the responsibility to make things happen. Look at the word "responsibility" - "response-ability." It can be understood as the ability to choose your response to situations.

People who create massive results recognize this responsibility not as a burden but as a power. They leverage this power to glide over the circumstances and opinions of other people. They develop a strong immune system to the negativity around them and remain unscathed. They do not blame circumstances, conditions, or conditioning for their behavior. Their behavior is a product of their own conscious choice based on values, rather than of their conditions based on feeling. For them, the flame of this inner power never extinguishes.

Some of your circumstances may be beyond your control, while you can change some others. You can live and operate under the shadows of things that you cannot change. Or you can look at things that you can impact and focus your thoughts and energy on moving those things. When you focus on things you cannot change, results don't come about, and you feel disempowered. Often people who do this state reasons for lack of movement as factors that are external to them. They blame others, their fate or destiny. People who choose to focus on things that are in their control and choose not to be too perturbed by things that aren't in their control, keep the power inside of them. This in turn makes them feel empowered and in control of their choices and actions. While the external environment may still not be fully under their control, they continue moving ahead and take actions in the areas where they can stride forward. This helps them move out of the static zone. And when this happens over a consistent period, they disentangle themselves out of the problems and make a way for themselves. They make it happen.

Would you be interested in knowing how to overcome your problem now? How you respond to your circumstances is a matter of choice. And that choice is always with you. What choice are you making today? Are your choices in line with your ability, or are your choices reflecting the challenges that you perceive around yourself? Will you keep fretting over them, or would you rather work on what is under your control?

Remember, you have the ability to respond. That is your responsibility towards success.

Exploring Your Full Potential

"How fast does it go?" Maya quizzed from the back seat.

"It doesn't matter," Rohan smirked, turning back to wink at her.

"Why?" she asked curiously.

He burst out laughing. "Because he is driving it," he said pointing at me. And I laughed along with them.

People who have traveled with me in my car would describe me as a cautious driver. And my so-called caution has been observed to be consistent, irrespective of the country or terrain that I am driving in. I don't drive slowly, but I don't drive fast either. So was the case, on this Sunday afternoon, when I took my friends for a drive in my new car. I had bought a new car, which had a powerful engine. The car was loaded with features and could rev up in a matter of seconds. I distinctly remember the salesperson at the car showroom telling me, "When you hit top speed, the car feels like it is floating on the road." While my driving habits were the center of the jokes that afternoon, it made me think.

I was driving at a speed that was significantly lower than the car's capacity. While I was driving slowly, the capacity of the car did not reduce. It could still easily go 230 miles per hour or more. We were on the freeway for a while, which had a speed limit. We then drove on a country road full of bumpy patches, and my speed reduced further. All the while, the car's capacity was constant. I chose to utilize only a fraction of it, sometimes due to the external road conditions and the other times due to my internal mechanism of caution.

If we draw a parallel of this to the pursuit of our dreams and desires, we will realize that we rarely utilize our full potential. Our internal engines have immense capacity, but a major part of it remains unused through our lifetimes. It is important to remember that just because we do not realize the capacity or have not used it, does not mean it has reduced.

In our journey toward success, we may have passed over a bumpy road or may have encountered a setback that instilled a sense of caution in us. But the potential remains. Often, the results that we manifest are commensurate to the potential that we have leveraged. To create maximum results, one must leverage the potential which remains hidden inside of us. Excavate your true potential. Rev it up.

Part IV – The Maximum Results Method

"There is no man living who isn't capable of doing more than he thinks he can do."

- Henry Ford

9. Embarking on The Voyage

Creating Results That Matter

If I ask you if money was not a constraint, which car would you like to own? Would you call out "If money were not a constraint, I would like a Chevrolet Spark?" That is unlikely. You may ask for a Bugatti Chiron or a Lamborghini Sian. The same goes for other areas of your life. Would you ever say, "If given a choice, I am ok being overweight and living with lack of sleep"? Or "I am ok with an average job for the rest of my life? I don't mind burning the midnight oil doing meaningless tasks at work"? The chances are you wouldn't.

If I ask you what kind of life you dream about, what would be your answer? I am sure your answer will depict the best that you can have. We all want the best in our life, and rightly so. However, the reality is that a lot of people end up settling for less. They make peace with modest results. There is absolutely nothing wrong with living a humble life. A lot of us have come from very humble backgrounds. However, it is ok only if you desire it. I am not suggesting that we all become paranoid and chase materialistic desires. All I am proposing is that you don't have to settle for mediocre, average results in any area of your life. The framework that we are about to explore will help you overcome your barriers to create results in your sphere which would be in line with your desires and would be significantly above average.

One would agree that the proposition of achieving maximum results has an energy to it and attracts attention. The picture that your mind may conjure may be of millionaire success routines, or of hitting a jackpot, winning a lottery, getting a million dollars in inheritance, etc. All of these are like getting hit by a bolt of lightning. It is important to temper our expectations. People who create maximum results do it as an outcome of consistent effort and a lot of patience. They do not enter the ring expecting a knockout in the first move. You may think that you are already working hard but have not yet seen the results. Creating such results requires something else as well. It requires a system that enables these results.

Reigniting Yourself

Marcus Aurelius was a Roman emperor and a Stoic philosopher. He was the last emperor of the Pax Romana, an age of relative peace and stability for the Roman Empire. He once said:

"Your principle can't be extinguished unless you snuff out the thoughts that feed them, for it is continually in your power to reignite new ones. It's possible to start living again! See things anew as you once did – that is how to restart life!"

For you to create results that you have never created before, you need to start seeing things the way you have never seen them before. You need to do things that you may not have done before. To move ahead, you need to break the chains of past results, which have tied you down. Your past can have a limited bearing on your future, but only if you desire it, think about it, and act accordingly. Restart your expedition.

Science experiments show us that iron has magnetic properties. Without magnetization, the piece of iron cannot even move a feather. However, if you enable its magnetic property by passing an electric current through the piece, it can lift things twelve times its weight. This is a maximum result – a result that is significantly beyond expectations. As Aurelius points out, it is in your power to reignite and enable the breakthrough properties within you. Reclaim your power.

A couple of years ago, I read a quote that made me think deeply.

"Don't wish it was easier, wish you were better. Don't wish for less problems, wish for more skills. Don't wish for less challenge, wish for more wisdom."

I invite you to imbibe this message, so beautifully articulated by Jim Rohn. As you read through the balance of this book, you will find a framework that will help you take the right steps towards achieving your desires. These are the success habits of super achievers. Here is to the newfound wisdom!

The Teacup

I was told that the traditional tea ceremonies are a must-do when visiting Japan. Apart from the aromatic Jasmine tea, what caught my attention was the teacup. Each of the teacups was unique, with its cracks and chips, while all being a part of the same set. It was evident that the artist had made them, using his own bare hands rather than a mold. My cup had interesting crevices, and it seemed like the artist had made peace with them and hence left them like that.

A little exploration got me to the concept of Wabi-Sabi, a part of Zen philosophy. *Wabi* refers to "simplicity" while *Sabi* refers to "taking pleasure in imperfection." These are evident in the way they have shaped the Japanese culture. The thought revolves around "imperfections." Wabi-Sabi is not an excuse for mediocre efforts or bad products. The key philosophy proposes the embrace of imperfections and making the most of what is there. Hence the potter accepts the natural crevices and chooses to leave them as they are in the cup.

While the concept of Wabi-Sabi is better understood with an inclination towards aesthetics, it is equally relevant in the sphere of self-awareness. Wabi-Sabi encourages us to look beyond our definitions and perceptions about how things should be perfect in our life as well as with us. Landon Donovan once said, "Life isn't perfect, of course, but we all know it's how you react to things that counts." When we don't wait for all circumstances to be perfect for us to act, we take charge of our lives. Embrace yourself and what you have in your life. No matter if it has crevices and cracks. Move ahead, the future is waiting for you.

The Invitation

"Do not believe in anything simply because you have heard it. Do not believe in anything simply because it is spoken and rumored by many. Do not believe in anything simply because it is found written in your religious books. Do not believe in anything merely on the authority of your teachers and elders. Do not believe in traditions because they have been handed down for many generations. But after observation and analysis, when you find that anything agrees with reason and is conducive to the good and benefit of one and all, then accept it and live up to it."

- Buddha

The subsequent chapters will reveal a system, a method, a framework, which when applied leads to the achievement of maximum results. How do I know it? The framework came into being based on my work with thousands of individuals in the capacity of coach, consultant, and observer. Over time, the practices that worked beyond expectations took the shape of a framework. This system, when consistently applied with the relevant skills and persistence of efforts, leads to results irrespective of the nature of the goals.

The framework consists of five unique dimensions. Each one of them is equally important to be worked upon. Imagine it is like a solar system with five planets. You are the creator, at the center of this solar system. The system works on the lines of a ripple effect. Your thoughts and actions expand across your sphere outwards. It works like a force multiplier and amplifies the effect.

As you go through the next chapters detailing each of these dimensions, I invite you to go further beyond just understanding them. Apply the insights before you move ahead. You need to conquer the bridge between insights and action. It is only then that you will hit a breakthrough.

10. Focusing Your Attention

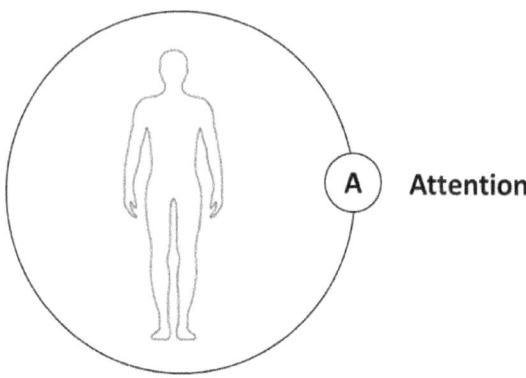

The First Dimension

Attention is the first of the five dimensions. The dimension of attention requires you to identify the realm in which you want breakthroughs to happen and to tap into the energy of that realm.

The Realms of Life

Imagine you are taking a ride in a hot air balloon. You are wondering what part of the town you are hovering over. You also recollect that one of your friends stays somewhere on this side of town. If you were to spot your friend's house and explain the directions to go to their house, while you are at an altitude of several thousand feet in the air, you may find it difficult. You may find it challenging to plot your friend's house, as all the houses look similar from that height. Your directions may be vague and lack direction, primarily because you would not have a proper line of sight from that altitude. Everything on the ground will look very small and incomprehensible as if all the things have been collapsed into a very small space. Distinguishing one from the other would be very difficult.

If I ask you "How is your life going?" what would your answer be?

You may respond by saying, "It is going great" or "It's going ok" or "Don't ask." There can be many more responses to this question, however, your answer may give a sense of what you are currently experiencing in your life.

If I then ask you, "Tell me more about it," what would your answer be?

You may share more about what is going on in your life. Some details may emerge across key areas of your life. The content will become specific. It is as if we narrowed the view from the balloon at an altitude of 1000 feet to closer to the ground. Working on results also requires narrowing our focus to specific areas of our life.

The structure of our life essentially comprises 5 primary realms. Each of these primary realms has sub-realms in them.

- Career, Business, and Vocations – This realm comprises the aspects of action and "what you do." This includes your profession and recreation.
- Health, Wellness, and Spirituality – This realm covers the aspects of the physical, mental and spiritual elements of your life.
- Love and Relationships – This realm focuses on your relationships with self, significant others, and community, as well as non-living elements such as nature.
- Finances – This realm covers aspects of money, investments, and life capital.
- Personal growth and Education – This aspect comprises aspects of your mindset, skills, and behaviors.

When we share our aspirations and desires in life, with statements such as "I want my life to be great," we lack specificity. The statements remain vague, like the directions from the hot air balloon. Achieving maximum results requires expectations that are specific and razor-sharp. To start with, identification of the realm of life in which you want to achieve the results is important.

Point for Reflection

The Realm Audit:
Conducting a realm audit can help unearth parts of your life terrain which need you to work upon them. Here is a simple exercise to help you conduct a realm audit for your life.

Step 1: Column 1 in the table below lists the primary realms of your life. Write down your vision for your life for each of the realms in column 2. Vision can also be understood as the "desired" or "to-be" state in that realm.

Step 2: In column 3, list the specifics about the reality as of now in that realm. Reality can also be understood as the "current" or "as-is" state in that realm.

Step 3: Look at the distinction between the vision and reality for each of the five realms. Observe your thoughts about the current reality, as well as the delta between reality and vision, for each of the realms. Write down your thoughts for each of the realms, in column 4.

Step 4: You can now choose either one or multiple realms for implementing the framework.

Realm	Vision	Reality	Thoughts
Career, Business and Vocations			
Health, Wellness and Spirituality			
Love and Relationships			
Finances			
Personal growth and Education			

Decoding Thoughts and Attention

The human brain is a unique organ. Despite accounting for only 2% of the body weight, the brain consumes around 20% of the energy used by the body. The reason is that the brain is responsible for cognition. Thinking, as a mental process, helps us assimilate and make sense of vast amounts of information that we come across every day. It aids in creating a view or a model of the world around us and decides upon our actions in their context. Thoughts are products of the thinking process. While the process of generation of individual thoughts is still an area of intense research in neuroscience, it has been established that each thought is unique and is a representation of something. Every time we experience an external stimulus, e.g. listening to the phone ring or watching an object move, it triggers a series of signals in our brain. These signals are in the form of electrochemical impulses. Essentially, our thoughts are a form of energy.

Attention, on the other hand, is understood as the concentration of awareness on something while excluding something else. When you watch the news on TV, you are paying attention to what the anchor is saying and are not aware of what is happening outside the window. There are three key traits of attention:

1. Our brain is wired to conserve energy. When we pay attention to something, the brain consumes more energy to decipher the event. This is also the reason why you may feel exhausted after looking at a lot of data or trying to follow lengthy instructions. In response, our brain tries to establish patterns so it can move the deciphering process to auto-pilot mode. This helps take off the attention and save energy.

2. Attention is controlled by two factors. The external environment is the first factor. The environment around us stimulates our senses, which guides our attention. E.g. a loud noise or a sweet smell may capture your attention. The second factor is the

choice of the individual. The person individually may choose to focus his or her attention on something at will.

3. Wherever attention goes, the brain follows. You can perceive it as, if your brain is the car, attention is the steering wheel. When you pay attention to something, the brain's processing ability is focused on it.

Quantum theory helps us understand the behavior of matter at atomic or subatomic levels i.e. the smallest level of energy. An experiment known as the Double Slit Experiment, conducted by Physicists Clinton Davisson and Lester Germer, showed that the behavior of particles can be changed just by observing them. Thoughts are a form of energy. When you start concentrating your attention on certain thoughts, you start tapping into their energy. The act of paying attention and observing your thoughts can significantly alter them, as well as your state of being.

The Great Law of Consciousness

"As within, so without; As above, so below."

This maxim comes from the philosophical tradition of alchemy and is attributed as the great law by

Hermes Trismegistus. The lines highlight the significance of the role of the subconscious in our thinking processes: whatever you impress in your subconscious mind becomes expressed on the screen of space. While these lines were written in Hermetica centuries ago, modern neuroscience substantiates these findings.

Before we experience a conscious thought, a lot of processing happens inside the subconscious brain behind the scenes. Our subconscious acts as a massive warehouse of thoughts and patterns. These thoughts, once generated, continue to remain stored within the subconscious just as they were input. We also relate to them as experiences and memories. The more highly emotionalized the thoughts when they were input, the deeper they are stored.

When you place your attention on a particular thought, your subconscious draws out a similar thought from its filing system. Have you ever noticed that when you start thinking about a sad memory or a difficult event, you jump from that thought to another sad thought and another one? These thoughts may or may not be related to each other, but they are similar in terms of the emotions that they generate. We have all learned the tenets of Kinetic theory in the elementary grades – "matter expands when heated." It is analogous to when you concentrate your attention on a particular thought, it triggers a chain reaction of thoughts, generating similar emotions.

Protection from Rust

In the seventeenth century, Luigi Galvani, an Italian physicist and biologist, invented a method that could prevent iron from rusting. He protected the iron plate by covering it in a layer of Zinc and, thus, the process of galvanizing was born. To this day, it forms the basis of modern efforts of preventing iron from rusting.

According to research conducted by Professor Alison Ledgerwood of the University of California, we experience crests and troughs of happiness and disappointments, depending on our experiences. While the blips of happiness last for some time, the disappointments continue to linger in our thoughts for much longer. As Professor Ledgerwood suggests, once we think about something as a loss, that way of thinking about it tends to stick in our heads and resists our attempts to change it. Our view of the world has a fundamental tendency to tilt toward the negative. It is very easy to go from good to bad, but far harder to shift from bad to good. We have to work harder to see the upside of things.

Ratan Tata, the former chairman of the Tata Group, once said, "None can destroy iron, but its own rust.

Likewise, no one can destroy a person but one's own mindset can." To achieve maximum results, we need to protect our thinking from its rust of negative thoughts, which induce doubt, fear, and anxiety. This requires a process like the one invented by Galvani. So, how can one galvanize their thinking?

Positive Distraction:

If you visit a bank, you will notice hefty armed guards at the entrance of the bank, protecting the bank and monitoring the people for any suspicious activity. Understandably so, as the bank has money and many precious belongings. Our mind is like the bank. It has many vital belongings, but unfortunately, it does not have a guard who can detect any suspicious activity or information entering our brain. We also realized earlier in this chapter that thoughts lead to similar feeling thoughts. A thought which sneaks into our brain, generating a feeling of fear, anxiety or doubt, can trigger a chain reaction of similar thoughts. This can lead to a significant change in the emotional state of the person. This makes the challenge even more compounded. However, our brain has a unique power that can help address both these risks: the power to selectively focus attention. When you choose to focus your attention on thoughts that generate a positive feeling, you take away the power of the unwanted thought and stop it from causing a chain reaction. A positive distraction is a process of shifting your attention consciously to positive thoughts. While this may seem like avoiding the situation, it is not. The deflection of thoughts helps you not get stuck in the spiral of negativity. It transports you temporarily into a different mental space, which helps you to refocus and move in a space of a more empowering mindset. You can then look at the problem or circumstance at hand in a more balanced and grounded manner. When you recognize that you are observing a negative thought, take a pause. Distract yourself with a better feeling thought.

The "Do" Focus:

That Friday, my schedule looked great. I had a few meetings during the day and then a coaching session. As the clock hit 3:00 p.m., Jerry was standing in front of me. I had always admired his punctuality. As we settled down, I noticed that he was in a different zone today, as if he were ruminating on something. That made me curious. Even before I could ask anything, he started.

"I feel I am stuck in this role. I don't want to keep doing this for the rest of my life. I have been doing this for years now. I don't want to wake up one day and feel that I have wasted my life. I don't want that feeling in me. I have thought hard about this. The time has come. I have thought about it and I don't want to rethink my decision. I don't want to do this anymore."

I noticed the emotional charge in him. I asked him, "Ok. I heard about what you don't want. What have you thought about what you want?" A long pause filled the room. It was as if lightning had struck him. He went blank as he grappled with thoughts in response to my question.

This was not a unique instance. Often, I have observed people talking incessantly about what they don't want. Sometimes they lack awareness of what they do want, or at times, they don't talk about it enough. When you constantly talk about what you don't want, you are focusing your attention on the presence of a problem, giving it momentum. That builds, leading you to questions like "Why is this happening? Why me? When will this be sorted out?" As you can see, all of these are disempowering thoughts. Instead, if you think about what you do want, you give energy to that thought. It leads you to the question of "What can I do to get it?" and helps you move ahead. Focus your thoughts on " What you do want" rather than "What you don't want."

A Dose of Optimism

According to Shawn Achor, a researcher at Harvard, the future success of individuals is influenced by their optimism as well as whether they view a challenge as stress or an impetus to improve. According to other research conducted by M. Laguna, G. Alessandri & G. V. Caprara on positive or negative orientation covering a set of entrepreneurs, more optimistic people tend to feel better about their goals than those with a more negative outlook. Both of these insights highlight the importance of optimism in achieving maximum results. It also leads to reduced anxiety and stress and promotes wellbeing. When you think about your previous successes, it fuels your optimism. Recollections of overcoming past challenges and achieving significant results can provide the right dose of sustained optimism to approach new goals. Maintaining a "Win Journal" can also go a long way. You can list your wins, no matter large or small, in a journal and keep it handy. Whenever you need a dose of optimism, flip through your journal to notice all the wins that you have had and all the challenges that you have overcome. It will immediately shift the energy of your thoughts.

Point for Reflection

Step 1: Revisit the Realm Audit that you conducted earlier in this chapter. Notice the thoughts that you have listed for each of the realms.

Step 2: Identify the thoughts that are negative and that you need to work upon.

Step 3: Explore the 3 techniques given in the preceding section for shifting attention from negative to positive thoughts. Identify what actions you can take to implement these techniques to address the negative thoughts. List the actions in the last column.

Realm	Vision	Reality	Thoughts	Actions
Career, Business and Vocations				
Health, Wellness and Spirituality				
Love and Relationships				
Finances				
Personal growth and Education				

Meteorological studies tell us that heat from the Sun warms up our environment. The difference in the pressure causes winds to flow from cooler areas to warmer areas. The bigger the difference, the faster the flow of wind. Imagine if you could do this with your thoughts as well. The warmth created by your attention to positive thoughts can change the direction of the winds of success in your favor.

Tip: Complete the two reflection exercises on Realm Audit and Attention on Thoughts before you move ahead to the next chapter.

11. Creating Powerful Intentions

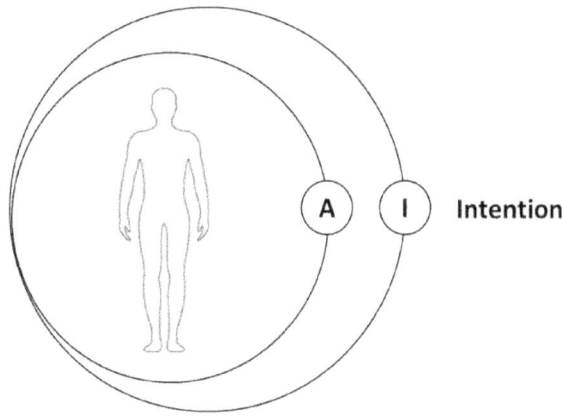

The Second Dimension

Castles in the Air

One afternoon, Todd received a letter. He grew curious as he never received any letters. It bore the news of his step-uncle passing away, and it also summoned Todd to the village beyond the river, where his uncle used to stay. The step-uncle had left his farm as an inheritance to his only relative, Todd. When Todd reached his uncle's village, the pastor showed him the farm and the house next to it. "It is yours now," he suggested. Todd was delighted looking at the large patch of the farm. His heart fluttered as he started imagining reaping a big crop of barley and then selling it to make a fortune. Weeks became months. Todd sat on the deck every day looking at the big farmland and rejoicing the dreams of the fortune awaiting him. One day, the pastor passed by, saw Todd sitting, and asked how it was going. Todd explained his plan to sow barley and reap a fortune. "But Fall is approaching. You have missed the season, my dear boy," the Pastor said. Suddenly, Todd's castles in the air came tumbling down.

A lot of us, like Todd, indulge in a tendency to daydream. We create lofty ideas of what we will achieve in our lives. While these daydreams entice us, they lack passion. Another form of daydreams is the "One day I will..." thoughts. They fail to generate enough momentum within us to take action. And so, these daydreams remain what they are, just wishful thinking. They never transform into reality. But why do we daydream?

Research by Elinor Amit at the Harvard Medical School shows that visual thinking is deeply ingrained in the human brain while speech is a relatively recent evolutionary development. People tend to create visual images to accompany their inner speech when they are prompted to verbalize their thoughts. We think in the form of images. The human brain creates patterns based on the information that it collects. These patterns are usually in the form of maps or images. Essentially, we think in the form of visual mental imagery. We convert these mental images into words and sentences to describe them. When we think of our desires, certain mental images pop up in our brains. These patterns have also made their way into our language and the way we express our thoughts. The use of visual language is prominent in our questions and expressions, e.g. "How does the future look?" or "I can see myself exercising every day."

Converting Images into Actions

William James, an American philosopher and psychologist, once said, "If you form a picture in your mind of what you would like to be, and you keep and hold that picture there long enough, you will soon become exactly as you have been thinking." While this statement has been interpreted by psychologists and healers in many ways, it highlights the importance of the visual elements of our thinking. Considered the father of American psychology, James proposed that consistent visualization could help achieve results.

When we think of our desires, we create mental images that depict these desires. Intentions are such powerful visions of our desired future, which fuel us with massive resolve. Intentions are distinct from daydreams. While daydreams are also visualizations, they lack the energy required to overcome our inner inertia to take action.

The key to achieve maximum results is to depict the desires in the form of powerful visual intentions. These intentions, when visualized consistently and unequivocally, create a drive for achievement. You feel empowered and in control. When our intentions lack this resolve, they remain meager daydreams, leading to either no action or a lack of wholehearted attempt to achieve what we want. The essence is in the way we represent our desires and thoughts.

Receiving It Versus Creating It

At the end of World War II, Japan was amidst the turmoil. The economy had crashed, and resources were scarce. One such resource which witnessed acute shortage was gasoline. Like everyone else, Soichiro Honda was struggling to feed his family. The times had become dire. Instead of feeling depressed, he created a powerful intention, of coming out of the situation and taking care of his family. His intention, fueled by the intense desire, made him ask himself, "What can I do to move ahead?" He came up with an idea to attach a small motor to his bicycle, creating the first motorbike. He drove his motorbike around, invoking interest from his friends and acquaintances. He continued with his powerful intention and made modifications to his invention, making it lighter and easier to ride. His efforts paid off, and his motorbike became a success. The business grew to become Honda Motor Company, as we know it today.

Sometimes, we find ourselves surrounded by circumstances which we may not perceive as favorable. When we let these circumstances determine our standing in life, we act from the role of the receiver. When surrounded by difficulty, we play the victim who is receiving whatever the circumstances may offer. When we take accountability for our life, we act from the role of the creator. Irrespective of what the circumstances offer, we create the life we desire. We empower ourselves, just like Mr. Honda did. Setting powerful intentions helps us make this shift from being the receiver to becoming the creator of our life.

Find Your Goliath

A visit to Florence is incomplete if you do not see the masterpiece by the renaissance artist, Michelangelo. The statue of David is a renowned sculpture created by Michelangelo in early 1500. David, as known in the biblical books, was a young shepherd who gained fame first as a musician and later by killing the enemy's champion. The battle between David and Goliath has been a timeless legend and has served as a tale of a contest where a smaller, weaker opponent faces a much bigger, stronger adversary.

The large piece of marble which was chosen for creating this sculpture of David was deemed a challenge not just by artists but also by the Opera authorities who had commissioned it. The block of stone rightfully so was named "the Giant." When Michelangelo started working on the sculpture, other sculptors denounced it as impossible. Legend has it that Michelangelo visualized that David was already in the marble and that he simply had to chip away the excess to allow him to emerge. His intention was so powerful that the 17-foot statue, once complete, was deemed structurally perfect by the world's best artists and sculptors. Michelangelo had achieved the impossible. Such is the intensity of powerful intentions.

The master artist once said, "The greater danger for most of us lies not in setting our aim too high and falling short, but in setting our aim too low and achieving our mark." His quests of sculpting David and painting the Sistine Chapel were proof of his sound belief in his intentions of achieving the impossible. When people feel diminished due to a lack of hope, they set their intentions too low. They accept the smallness of the expectations and make do with mediocre results. They do not utilize the leverage of powerful intentions. Default intentions lead to default results. Maximum results require powerful intentions. Find your Goliath and conquer it.

How Badly Do You Want It?

In Norse mythology, Asgard, the fortress of the Gods, was believed to rest on the upper branches of the great tree, Yggdrasil. Once, three powerful maidens created carvings in the tree's trunk, which defined the destiny of the world. Odin, the widely revered God of war and the father of Thor, grew curious. He wanted to know what the carvings depicted but did not know how to. He knew that the carvings would reveal themselves only to someone who proved their worthiness to them. With every passing day, Odin felt the intensity only growing. He wanted wisdom at any cost. Driven by his burning desire, Odin pierced himself with a spear and hung himself on the tree. Odin continued to focus on the carvings for nights and days in that state. Moved by Odin's unrelenting hunger, the carvings revealed themselves. Odin wielded wisdom and many other powers to become the great God.

One may surmise that even Gods must desire their need intensely to yield it. Antonie De Saint-Exupery once said, "If you want to build a ship, don't drum up people to collect wood and don't assign them tasks and work, but rather teach them to long for the endless immensity of the sea." The wisdom running through the ages recognized that longing is the key to the puzzle.

Sir Issac Newton was an English mathematician and physicist and is recognized as one of the most influential scientists of all time. He crafted the three laws of motion, which form the foundation of modern-day mechanics. Newton's second law states that the rate of change of velocity of an object is directly proportional to the force applied and takes place in the direction of the force. If you apply this law in the given context, it would lead to two implications:

1. The higher the intensity of your intention, the more the resolve it carries to move you in the right direction.

2. The speed with which you move into action is directly dependent on how badly you want it.

The key question is, How badly do you want to achieve your results?

The Pink Elephant

Let's play a small game of imagination. Take a moment to imagine the things listed below, as you read further along.

Imagine a lemon.

Now, imagine a basket full of apples.

Imagine your favorite dessert.

Now, imagine a pink elephant.

How was the experience? The chances are that you could visualize these things without any difficulty. What do we realize from this simple exercise?

Your brain is an incredible powerhouse that can imagine and project vivid images on command. Your brain can do all of this in a fraction of a second. We all are visual beings. We first like to visualize and then act. Visuals are like maps for us. They guide our actions and fuel the energy to act in that direction. We conjure up all this energy and move ahead.

Going back to the imagination game, you will notice that your brain also filled in some missing details of the visual. The exercise did not specify the color of the lemon. Your brain retrieved it from its extensive databank of existing knowledge stored within. It also did not specify the number of apples in the basket or the type of the basket. While the chances are that different people may have seen a different number of apples, their brains will have plugged in the missing information. Let's go further. When I ask the participants in my workshop to imagine their favorite dessert, they have reported that often they salivate just thinking about it. That tells us that an electrochemical reaction is triggered inside your brain in response to the visuals you project, and your body generates a physiological response. And all of it happens based on an imaginary visual.

When I asked you to visualize a pink elephant, the image of an elephant is stored in your brain, but imagining it pink required some effort on the part of the brain. While some can do it in the first go, some may need 2-3 attempts, but they will be able to visualize a pink elephant. No matter how unrealistic it may seem what you are trying to imagine or visualize, your brain has the capacity to do it. And not just do it vaguely but with specificity and full detail.

Sometimes this ability of our brain remains untapped because we are too caught up with what we think is realistic. And we draw the same yardstick for our goals, desires, and dreams. Ask yourself if you have ever parked a desire to reach your dream because you thought it was unrealistic for you to achieve. It might have been difficult, and you may not have known how to achieve it. And hence you thought it was unrealistic. This stops us from even visualizing it, let alone thinking about ways to achieve it.

We need to use the untapped ability of our brains to visualize our goals, desires, and pursue dreams. It may take some time and effort, but it is possible.

Power of Visualization

We visualize all the time. Our brain is constantly thinking and projecting mental images. Sometimes we are conscious of it. Often, it happens unconsciously. When our mental images are of positive things, our emotions elevate, and we feel energized and relaxed. However, when we visualize challenges, our emotions take the form of fear, anxiety, doubt, or anger. We feel a sense of stress in the body and our physiological response. Research conducted at the University of Nevada, Las Vegas, indicated that a guided visualization practiced by the study participants lowered levels of perceived stress, as well as lowered psychological and physical complaints. Another research conducted in 2005 by Dr. Elisha Goldstein demonstrated that study subjects who spent 5 minutes a day practicing a guided visualization and meditation exercise reported significantly reduced stress levels and enhanced feelings of well-being compared to control subjects.

When we visualize things consciously, we fuel them with intent. To visualize something is to see it in our mind's eye as if it were alive right now. You create powerful intentions by creating a strong visualization of your desires. Making the visual compelling is very important. It must be so powerful that it moves you. It should energize your being. When you consistently visualize something, new neural connections are created in your brain and the more real the visuals appear to you. The more real it seems, the more likely you are to pursue it with consistent effort. You can condition your mind through this conscious and consistent repetition.

Point for Reflection

Here is a step-by-step Visualization exercise for creating powerful intentions:

Step 1: Find a comfortable spot where you can do this exercise without being disturbed. Sit comfortably and close your eyes. Take 3 deep breaths – inhale and exhale from the bottom of your stomach. Calm your mind.

Step 2: Keep your eyes closed. Think about the life realm in which you want to create results. You can refer to the Life Realm Audit exercise done in the previous chapter.

Step 3: Create a mental image of your ideal state in this realm. Visualize how it would look. The idea is not to create a list of desired attributes but to see it.

Step 4: While continuing to keep your eyes closed, turn on the intensity of the visual. Imagine it playing like a movie in front of your eyes. Include the details – what you are doing in the visual, the surroundings, the colors, the sounds, the smells, etc. Don't worry about the possibility of it happening or how will it happen. Just visualize it and enjoy the experience. Notice your feelings while you are visualizing. If you are feeling happy, joyous, and excited, you are doing it right.

Step 5: Once the visual is complete in your mind, gently open your eyes. Write down your visual on a piece of paper, describing what you saw, heard, and felt. It is key to write it down using positive words and in the present tense as if it is currently happening. E.g. I am sitting on the deck of my farmhouse, reading my favorite book. The sun is shining beautifully, and I can feel the gentle loving breeze on my skin….

Step 6: Repeat the visualization exercise every day, once after you wake up and once before you go to sleep. Remember to do it intently and feel it completely. If you can, read the visualization aloud at least once every day.

Point of No Return

In 1519 AD, Hernán Cortés, the Spanish knight-explorer, led an expedition that caused the fall of the Aztec Empire and brought large portions of what is now mainland Mexico under the rule of the king of Spain. He led an armada of 11 ships and 500 men to wage the annexation. Engulfed by his intense desire to win the war, he ordered the deliberate sinking of the ships as soon as the armada hit the coast. This left him and his men with no other choice than to win. Eventually, they did.

Affirm to yourself, no matter what, you will make it happen. Rather than the audacity of your desires creating fear and doubt in you, let your powerful intentions be the wind in your sail.

No matter what.
Tip Create your powerful intentions for the chosen realm and practice visualization before you move ahead to the next chapter.

12. Generating Energy of Emotions

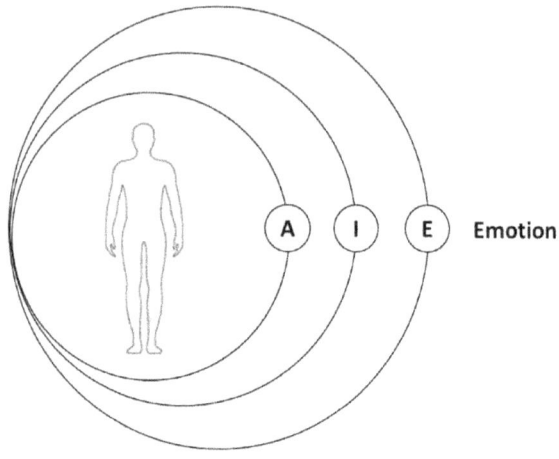

The Third Dimension

The Bite of 97

The lights flooded the MGM Grand Arena in Las Vegas. The crowd roared as the two warriors entered the ring. This great rematch, touted as the biggest bout of the time, was called "The Sound and the Fury." On June 28, 1997, the two heavyweights of boxing, Evander Holyfield and Mike Tyson, were ready to clash again. The first match had witnessed the underdog Holyfield winning a surprise victory by knocking out Tyson. It was intense due to the recent history between the two: Holyfield wanting to prove his mettle and Tyson wanting to reclaim his glory.

The fight began with Holyfield dominating Tyson. Holyfield won the initial rounds. In the second round, Holyfield ducked, and in doing so, he head-butted Tyson, opening a large cut over the latter's eye. In the third round, with forty seconds remaining, Tyson bit a part of Holyfield's ear off. After some debate, the match referee disqualified Tyson for the act and announced Holyfield the winner. The incident has been reported as one of the low points of boxing history. Later, Tyson in an interview with Fox News said, "I bit him because I wanted to kill him. I was really mad. I really lost consciousness of the whole fight." It was Tyson's anger which had made him act that way.

Emotions drive our behavior. Sometimes we realize it, sometimes we don't. In the previous chapter, we established the importance of thoughts. When we think about anything, it generates a feeling within us. This feeling, when intense, creates a physical response which is known as behavior. Every thought and decision of ours has an emotional intensity attached to it. The higher the intensity of the emotion, the higher the probability of action. Neuroscience research shows that people with damaged emotional centers in their brains do not act, even after identifying many reasons to do so. This is due to the absence of emotions to drive the actions.

Decoding Emotions

The word "emotion" finds its origin in the French word *émouvoir*, and dates back to the 1570's. The literal meaning of its French ancestor was "to stir up." Emotions do stir up something inside us, which makes us behave in certain ways. Emotions are complex phenomena. Many theories define what emotions are. Some state emotions as "experiences associated with physiological activities," whereas others define them as "states of feelings leading to physical and physiological changes, that influence behavior." Emotions are generated subconsciously and autonomously, in response to a stimulus, either external or internal. Feelings are our subjective experiences of the emotions, which are driven by our interpretations. When we experience a stimulus, emotions are generated. This leads to your brain releasing biochemicals or hormones, which then leads to physiological sensations.

Evolutionary scientists propose that emotions played a vital role in our evolution. Emotions drove the fight-or-flight responses of humans to keep them safe from danger. They were associated with the adaptive behaviors, used as a defense in response to a threat. While humans and their brains have significantly evolved, emotions continue to play a very vital role in our lives. They help us make choices and take decisions. Emotions guide the decision process, especially when there is no clear rational basis for the choice or in cases where the options seem to be very similar to each other.

The Hijack

Our brain processes huge volumes of data, identifies an appropriate response, and then triggers an action. Its response system can be understood as having two distinct parts. The first part is fast, driven by impulse, and decides on the response based on the feelings. Let's call it the "feeling" part of the brain. The second part is evaluative. It tries to identify patterns, analyze them, and deduce conclusions based on logic. This takes time, and hence it is slower compared to the feeling part. This logical part is known as the "thinking" part. The primary mode of our brain is the "feeling" mode.

When we experience a stimulus, our brain interprets it to make sense of it. Stimuli can be of two types: external and internal. An external stimulus can be a situation or an event experienced by us. An internal stimulus is usually our thoughts. Both these types of stimuli trigger the generation of emotions. Two parts within the brain play a significant role in this process. The amygdala, which is a collection of cells, gives meaning to the emotions and creates memories attached to the emotions. The frontal lobes are the rational, thinking systems within the brain that lead the decision-making process. When the brain experiences a strong stimulus which it perceives as threatening, the amygdala takes over the response system automatically, also known as the amygdala hijack. It releases hormones to alert the body of the fight-or-flight response. In such cases, usually, the outcomes are sudden, unanticipated, and irrational response behaviors. Tyson biting Holyfield's ear was an outcome of the amygdala hijack. One may guess that the fear of losing the match again had triggered it.

While some may think that emotions such as fear and anger are negative and best to be avoided, the reality may not support it. It is impossible not to experience emotions since they are automatically generated and one has little control over the process. Emotion is not negative or positive. The actions that we take in light of the experienced emotion either help us or derail us. It is critical to evaluate the context in which the emotion is being experienced. While anger is considered negative, a context in which one ought to be angry may not have negative effects. The so-called negative emotions, when channeled appropriately, can also help you. The emotion of fear, when used appropriately, can help you get over procrastination and laziness. It can help you move into action.

Emotions essentially are the fuel for action. Where you feed this fuel determines the outcome.

Point for Reflection

Step 1: Explore your memories of the recent past. Identify a situation where you may have experienced an amygdala hijack.

Step 2: Recall the incident and the chain of events.

Step 3: Identify the thoughts that were running in your mind and the inherent emotion which caused the amygdala hijack.

Step 4: Evaluate the thoughts to check for the facts and the perceptions.

The Grave Mismatch

Sometimes we experience a lack of congruity between what we want and what we feel. Our desires generate a sense of achievement and make us feel good. Thinking about the achievement of our goals makes us feel the positive emotion of joy. However, thinking about the seemingly difficult nature of the goals or the possibility of attainment generates doubt. Thoughts about failure cause fear within us. This dissonance can lead us to swing between emotional states like a pendulum. To move ahead, we need to remove or at least reduce, this dissonance to the extent possible. Until the same goal generates two polar emotions, one may not act with full will.

When you think of what you don't know and what may happen if you fail, it causes fear. Your survival instincts come into play when you experience emotions of fear. Your inner guidance tries to protect you from the perceived threat. Your adaptive behavior in this case is that of withdrawal or retreating from the action. When you think of how it will be when you succeed, you feel excited about the proposition. Your instincts nudge you to go out and explore the environment and the things that constitute it. The feeling of joy makes you move ahead and take the next steps.

The same goal or desire can generate multiple emotions in you. Leveraging your emotions in your pursuit is up to you. When you manage your emotions in a way that prompts you to act per your goal, it can help you gain significant momentum.

Point for Reflection

Step 1: Think about the realm in which you want to create results.

Step 2: Think about the specific results you want to achieve.

Step 3: As you think about these results, explore the various thoughts that come to your mind.

Step 4: Observe the emotions that are generated within you. Check if there is a dissonance.

Step 5: Shift your attention to desirable thoughts so that your emotional state also shifts accordingly.

Where is the Train?

I have distinct memories of traveling by train when I was young. I was not very fond of long travel, and I always wanted the journey to end sooner. One of the factors contributing to my lack of liking was the wait for the train to come. Sometimes, the announcements at the platform let you know about the possible arrival, but most times you had to patiently wait. I frequently went closer to the edge of the platform to check if I could see the train coming in. The line of sight was only up to half a mile, as the tracks curved beyond that distance and disappeared behind the buildings. The assurance would come only when I saw the train, once it crossed the curve. Until then, the impatient wait would continue.

Often, we feel similar anguish while waiting for our results to appear. We check our inbox frequently and wait for the call patiently. We coax ourselves and then find solace in quotes such as "Good things take time." When the results don't appear within our expected time, it leads to disappointment. The emotion of sadness starts gaining ground over this uncomfortable space between expectation and reality. Questions such as "Why has it not come yet?" and "Why is it taking so long?" crop up frequently. When this pause elongates, it leads to frustration and anger, risking a drastic decision of giving up or a feeling of indifference. These can sabotage the efforts put in so far to achieve the results.

One of the catchwords that stayed with me from my consulting days was "WIP." It was used to denote any work product which was not yet complete, a "work-in-progress." People would save files marking them as WIP. They would put forth recommendations to clients qualifying those as WIP. It was interesting to see how the acronym was also used to temper expectations in a way, that this was not the end product and should be judged only as the name suggests. While the term still is used largely as a disclaimer, I am fascinated by its potential in regulating the emotional states within us. When the way one feels is controlled by the happening of an external event, one cannot influence the event, since she or he is a part of it. But when you can control the way you feel in the event, you gather the ability to influence it. When you tell yourself that your results are work-in-progress, you can alleviate impatience and frustration. It uplifts your energy, instills belief, and helps you sustain your efforts. Some may think that this is giving an empty assurance to yourself. For a moment, let's go back to my childhood experience of waiting on the platform. Just because I could not see the train at that moment did not mean that it was stationary or not coming. It would appear at the right line of sight. Similarly, your results will show their signs once you reach the inflection point. Progress isn't always obvious. Frustration and anger caused by the wait for results can derail your efforts. Being in a state of positive anticipation can help you condition your mind for success. Positive anticipation is a state where you are expecting your results to come, without being impatient and frustrated about the time that it is taking for them to surface. Tell yourself the results are work-in-progress. The train is coming.

Calling the Wind

For centuries, sailing has been the hinge for the evolution and expansion of civilizations. Sailors used to set out on expeditions to span across continents, braving rough seas. Back in the day, it was the force of the wind, which was leveraged by ships to sail ahead. Sailors used to whistle pleasant melodies while sitting in the direction from which they wanted the wind to blow. As superstitious as it may sound, it was done to call a gust of wind which would help the sail.

Our emotions act as the tailwinds for our goals to move ahead. When our actions are supported by strong winds of our emotions, we take significant strides and cover a lot of ground. The question remains, how can you whistle the wind of emotions to help you set sail? You can do that by looking for reasons which make you feel good. In the previous chapters, we established how a thought attracts another thought of a similar feeling. When you think of something which makes you feel good, it attracts similar feeling thoughts. And very quickly, the gentle breeze turns into a strong gust. Start your day by looking for thoughts that make you feel good. Surround yourself with things that generate joy and happiness within you. The longer you focus on positive thoughts, the stronger the intensity of emotion becomes. And the more powerful is its effect.

The Spent Arrow

Idries Shah once said, "Three things cannot be retrieved - the arrow sped from the bow, the word spoken in haste, the missed opportunity."

You will recollect from the earlier chapters that we do not think in the form of words. We think in the form of images, and then we convert them into words. The spoken or written word is then used to communicate the thoughts. Similarly, when we receive words by reading or hearing them, the brain converts them into images to make sense of what is being shared. Let's do a small exercise. Imagine the following words one by one:

Turmoil

Difficulty

War

Riot

Each of these words may likely have created a unique image inside your brain. Similarly, when you speak, you project images back to your brain for it to interpret and store. When you use words such as "fail" or "failure," your brain creates an image and stores it. The next time you think about a similar experience, your brain will project this image since it has established that association. You will see an image of failure. Your language will follow suit, and so your actions will also adapt.

Our words have more impact on our thoughts and behaviors than we realize since they are all closely coupled. When you say, "I hope this happens," it has the tone of an inner doubt of the possibility of it happening. The tentativeness leads to a feeling of anxiety and grows into subtle fear. Instead, when you say, "it will happen," it projects certainty. The optimism makes you feel in control, and you are less likely to feel anxious about the outcomes. It is key to note that just empty words cannot lead to results. Of course, they need to be backed with the right action. When you replace words such as "would, could, should, try, hope" with anchor words such as "will, certainly, surely, without any doubt," your mind shifts the mental images inline, leading to a positive shift in your emotional state.

Point for Reflection

Step 1: Write down the recurring thoughts that you have regarding the results that you want to achieve.

Step 2: Underline the words that instill tentativeness in your actions and the possibility of results.

Step 3: Identify anchor words that instill certainty, which you can use to replace the underlined words.

Step 4: Practice using the new words in your narrative as frequently as you can.

Buddha's Smile

Research shows that there is a strong link between our thoughts and emotions, as well as the integrated behavior of our body. When you experience anger, you also experience a change in heart rate, blood pressure, and pulse. Every emotion that we experience has a bodily response. And it works the other way around, too. When you engage in any cardiovascular activity, your brain releases hormones that help you beat stress. A gentle caress or an embrace of a loved one can instantly shift one's emotional state. Research by Marsha Linehan, a psychologist at the University of Washington, in 1983 showed that when people altered their facial expressions on a purely muscular level, their emotions were affected, and so was activity in the nervous system associated with positive or negative emotions. Another study by psychologist Sarah Pressman of the University of California found that people who smiled while getting an injection at a doctor's clinic reported up to 40 percent less pain than people who didn't. That was even though they were essentially tricked into smiling by positioning chopsticks in their mouths.

Have you ever observed the peace and tranquility on the face of Buddha? It is also accompanied by what is known as a "half-smile." Half-smile is a unique technique used in Cognitive Behavior Therapy, or CBT. It has roots in ancient Buddhist practices and leverages the connection between the body and emotional states. As the name suggests, the half-smile is a subtle, small smile. To practice the half-smile technique, begin to smile with your lips, but stop just when you notice a small amount of tension at the corners of your mouth. Now, continue smiling in this way for around ten minutes. You will notice how your mood will make a positive shift. When you continue smiling, your body sends back signals to your brain. Your brain accordingly releases the hormones in line with the physiological changes of the body, and the emotional shift happens. In the same way, if you furrow your eyebrows and keep them that way for some time, you will experience tension and signs of anger. The half-smile is one of the easiest and quickest ways to shift your emotional state.

13. Leveraging Your Intuition

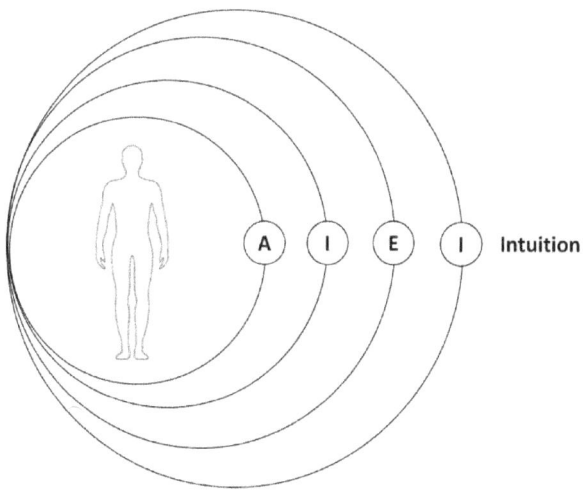

The Fourth Dimension

Eureka!

Archimedes, the great Greek mathematician and inventor, was once tasked by King Hiero to assess if the goldsmith had cheated in making his crown. He was suspected to have added some silver to the gold. Archimedes kept puzzling with the problem. During a subsequent trip to a public bath, he encountered a strange phenomenon. While taking the bath, an insight came to him as he noticed the rise in the water level of the bathtub. He figured out that the displaced water was an exact measure of his volume. He realized that using this insight, he could evaluate the volume of the crown and solve the problem. And he exclaimed "Eureka" in excitement.

Many people report that, like Archimedes, they receive ideas or flashes of insight while in the shower. Research conducted by scientist Scott Barry Kaufman highlighted that 72% of people covered in the study had experienced creative ideas while taking a shower. It suddenly makes the routine, daily activity of taking a shower enigmatic. This phenomenon may be explained to some extent through neuroscience. Let's look at what a shower typically provides us with: some solitude, distraction from the daily routine, and a way to relax. Research suggests that dopamine, a key hormone within the brain, is released while we take a relaxing shower. Dopamine is essential for creative ventures. This is supplemented by a lack of fixation of attention on any one thing. We give our brains those rare moments of solitude away from gadgets. While in the shower, the executive functions of the brain are temporarily paused, and the attention is relaxed. The parts of the brain which do the processing of data and the thinking functions take a backseat. However, brain scans depict that another part of the brain, the medial prefrontal cortex, responsible for associations and emotional response, steps up its activity while we shower. A relaxed state of mind, an influx of dopamine, the pause of the brain's critical thinking, and the solitude create the perfect setting. Like a flash of lightning, an insight or an idea appears inside our brain. When we are actively thinking to find a solution to a problem, our attention is directed outward. In the calming environment of the shower, our attention is directed inward, leading to the identification of new patterns and the arrival of an idea or insight. While several factors influence this, it highlights the presence of other mental faculties available to us apart from just critical thinking.

An Encounter of the "Third" Kind

In Hindu mythology, the pantheon of gods is led by the holy trinity: Lord Brahma, who created the universe; Lord Vishnu, who sustains it; and Lord Shiva, who resurrects it for it to be created again. For ages, Shiva has been represented as a mystic yogi, with legends about him being passed on for centuries. One such fable is that Goddess Parvati, who later became his consort, wanted to marry him, but Shiva was in deep meditation and absolute indifference. The gods persuaded Kamadeva, the god of love, to instill the desire in Shiva. Kamadeva shot a flowery arrow from his bow only to find Shiva angry for being disturbed. Shiva opened his third eye and burnt Kamadeva into ashes. While this depiction of the third eye of Shiva has been largely in the context of destruction, there is another known dimension to it. It is believed that Shiva, through his yogic dexterity, possessed cosmic knowledge, and his third eye represented that wisdom.

For centuries, the third eye has been depicted as a symbolic eye that sees what the other two eyes cannot. Our two eyes are focused outward and see the physical world. The third eye, depicted as placed between the eyebrows, is the one that focuses inward and sees what is beyond obvious. It is referred to as a gate to the inner depths of a higher order of consciousness. In Buddhism, the third eye is considered the vantage point from which enlightenment beyond the physical senses can be achieved. It provides access to knowledge that cannot be accessed through the intellect.

The Inexplicable Faculty

We have all experienced intuition at some of the other points in our lives, either in the form of inner guidance or a vision or a feeling to do or not do something. People at times try to verbalize it in the form of feelings or knowing – "It doesn't feel right" or "I know it will work." While we can mostly say what that guidance is, it is difficult to explain. The question around where this guidance comes from remains unanswered. While scientific progress has established some elements around intuition, a lot yet remains to be uncovered.

As humans, we have always given merit to rational thinking for arriving at decisions. Generation after generation, we have promoted thinking as the key faculty to survive and grow. However, often in the zeal to "think through" our decisions, we drown out the inner voice which can be useful guidance while taking decisions. Often, people dissuade themselves from paying any heed to their intuition because they are not able to explain why or how the guidance came about. Albert Einstein once said, "The intuitive mind is a sacred gift, and the rational mind is a faithful servant. We have created a society that honors the servant and has forgotten the gift." Just because we don't understand it fully yet does not mean we deny its existence or discourage ourselves from paying attention to it.

For centuries, thinkers have defined intuition as the awareness which cannot be acquired by either inferring or observing, neither by reasoning nor by experience. Intuition is often understood as a form of knowledge that one becomes aware of without conscious effort or deliberation. It is the ability to know something without conscious reasoning. It is not logical, and hence it is difficult to explain how one comes to know of it. People experience intuition in various forms: a thought, an idea, a specific feeling about something, a physical sensation like goosebumps, palpitation, or even the form of a dream. The form in which intuition will occur also cannot be generalized. People often construe these signs as instinct. Instinct, or instinctual response, denotes our predisposition towards a particular behavior that has been hardwired into our brain as a result of our evolution. It has a nature of if-then. For example, if you see a lion, then your response will be to run for your life.

While neuroscientists are further exploring this area, a hypothesis around intuition is that some dormant parts of the brain wake up temporarily in a particular environment to create connections. These connections appear as a sudden flash in the nervous system. When we experience this flash, it is difficult to explain where it came from, as the usual methods of the thinking processes are not followed.

Point for Reflection

Step 1: Recollect a situation from your recent past wherein you had a sudden flash of intuition. This could be a thought, a feeling, a physiological sensation, or any other form.

Step 2: Recollect your interpretation of the intuition. What was your intuition trying to tell you?

Step 3: Recollect your response to the intuition. Did you pay attention to it or ignore it?

Adventures of Banner and Hulk

Bruce Banner and the Hulk, the key characters in the superhero squad of the Avengers, depict a key duality of the human mind. Dr. Banner, a physicist, represents the thinking, evaluative and cautious side of the persona, while the Hulk represents the very powerful, instinct-led, self-preserving alter ego of Banner. Both exist within the same body but surface in different scenarios. While Banner seems to be in control most of the time, the Hulk emerges in situations that trigger intense emotions or a sense of danger. Our mind - the consciousness which exists through the processing of our brain - works similarly. The conscious mind is like Bruce Banner. It retains control of our awareness most of the time. Our subconscious is like the Hulk, which remains inside all the time but surfaces and makes its presence felt in specific situations, in response to certain stimuli.

Our conscious mind is the house of reasoning. It collects data through the five senses and interprets it to create patterns and inferences. Based on these inferences, it guides the response of the body through thoughts and physiological sensations. This process usually follows a predictable set of steps, which can be plotted via brain scans and tests. On the other hand, the subconscious mind houses emotions and memory. It is not reliant on the five senses to interpret the surroundings. The subconscious mind also processes its inputs and responds in the forms of feelings, hunches, physiological sensations, and flashes of thoughts. This is what we commonly term "intuition." Little is known about how these steps are processed as well as where they happen inside the brain. But one surely can tell the existence of this response.

Given it is involuntary, it becomes difficult to predict when the flash of intuition will strike. However, it is understood to mostly occur when certain conditions are prevalent. Flashes of intuition appear when the brain is not actively thinking about something. This rather suspended state, with an openness to receive, becomes the ideal ground for intuition to occur.

Why Intuit?

Often, we assume that insight is only worth it when it is conscious and a product of deliberate thinking. We have conditioned ourselves to look for insights in this manner, at times restricting our ability to unearth new pathways. Our brain is a very complex machine with an intricate and composite set of circuitries. The working of the human brain is still a difficult puzzle that many neuroscientists are attempting to solve. The brain is an immense powerhouse that has capabilities beyond reason. At times these are beyond the abilities of current scientific methods to interpret fully. Intuition is one such ability that we don't fully understand yet, however, we feel its presence occasionally.

A team of psychologists and scientists--Galang Lufityanto, Chris Donkin, and Joel Pearson at the University of New South Wales in Australia--researched in 2016 the role of intuition. Their research highlighted that intuition significantly benefited decision making and that nonconscious information increased decision accuracy, speed, and confidence. The findings suggested that people use unconscious information in the body or brain to help guide them through life, take better decisions, and be more confident about themselves. The research also highlighted that intuition improved over time, suggesting that the mechanisms of intuition can be improved with practice.

It is not recommended that you follow your intuition blindly. However, our intuition can supplement the rational thinking ability. It can supply us with insights that our conscious brain cannot. Individuals who attain a high level of self-awareness and mind control can compartmentalize their conscious and subconscious, opening doors for intuition to come in as needed. Intuition works as a guidance system, like GPS. When one has the insights derived from conscious thinking processes as well as intuition, he or she is leveraging the full potential of the brain. It is like having the full map of the expedition with additional callouts on which route to take. Often, we are faced with problems that seem insurmountable or a question for which no one has an answer. Intuition can be the faculty which, when leveraged, can help you overcome these.

It is key to remember that intuition is not magic. It is a faculty of your subconscious, which is the reservoir of feelings and storage of all memories. Just because you are not able to trace the steps of its origin, you should not ignore it. It is like enjoying a meal which is made by a chef you don't know and made in a kitchen you can't see a door to. The basic currency to be able to leverage your intuition is to develop a relationship of trust with it.

Activating the GPS

Your intuitive ability already exists deep within the hollows of your subconscious. The focus of your efforts should be first, to amplify it so that it becomes more noticeable, and second, to invite it when you need it. These may look unattainable at first glance, but the practices and techniques given below have proven to be effective in accomplishing this.

The practices and techniques for enabling intuition are of two types:

- Passive practices – These practices are aimed at preparing yourself to become more aware of the intuition, whenever it surfaces. You inherently wait for the guidance to come to you.
- Active practices – These practices are intended to create an environment that will attract intuition in more likelihood. It is as if you are setting the stage and inviting it to come.

Both these techniques are helpful and have their own merits. It is recommended to master the passive techniques first before you move on to the active techniques, as it will help you become more adept at inviting and noticing the intuition. Let's look at some of the passive practices first.

Observing the subtleties - The inner voice of intuition speaks in various ways. But whenever it does, it is important to notice it. Intuition is often subtle and may drown out in the noise of our internal thoughts and processing. Observing the finer changes in your emotional and physiological states can help you become more alert. It can occur as a flash of a visual, a thought, a sudden feeling, a voice or sound, a physical sensation, or any other form. Once you tune into your state, you will surely know the presence of it when it happens.

Being Open – While being open may not have a bearing on the flashes of intuition as it is understood to be an involuntary process, it can help you become more receptive. When you don't judge the quality of the insight or the way it is delivered, you are being more receptive to the occurrence of it. Not judging yourself as a party to the process and as a believer of intuition is also equally important.

Being in Solitude – Intuition comes only in the absence of active thought. Throughout our day, we are drowned in massive tides of information. Often, we hook ourselves to our mobile phones and smart gadgets whenever we get a moment. Intuition requires a calm state of mind which is not preoccupied with another thought. Practicing quiet solitude, away from gadgets and other people, provides that window for your intuition to make its presence felt. While being alone, don't focus your attention on anything in particular. Let yourself drift along with the flow.

Now that you have prepared yourself, let's look at the active techniques to invite your intuition.

Journaling – When you write down your thoughts, feelings, and physiological signals as they occur, you create a channel of expression for your intuition. A good practice is to sit with a blank journal and start writing or drawing whatever comes to your mind. It is key to not evaluate, analyze or rationalize them while writing or drawing them out. When you journal regularly without actively thinking about it, it provides an opening for your intuition to flow through you into your journal. Journaling your dreams can also help you open that channel for intuition to appear.

Asking Questions – Your intuition can fill the gaps in the insights generated by your active thinking. You can pose questions proactively to your subconscious mind with an expectation of retrieving the answers. It is key to note that one should not expect the answers to come in a certain way. We are used to speaking and understanding the language of our thoughts, which is spoken primarily by our conscious mind. Our subconscious may or may not speak that language. It may deliver your answers in a different language and being open to it is important.

Meditating – When you meditate, you let go of your active thoughts and transcend to a state of higher consciousness. You get in a flow and activate your subconscious. In a way, you open the gateways of your consciousness, inviting your intuition. Meditation requires deep practice. Your attention may stray initially, but with intentional and persistent efforts, you will be able to meditate well.

Sleeping on it – There is an adage, "The morning is wiser than the evening." We enter a very deep state of mind while we sleep. The conscious processing efforts of the brain hibernate temporarily, meaning that efforts of the subconscious take prominence. Amidst the peace of the night, your subconscious is better placed to deliver an intuitive insight as compared to the hustle-and-bustle of the day. You can pose questions to your subconscious or ask for help just before you go to bed. These active commands will process during your sleep, and your subconscious may provide you answers in the form of intuition.

Intuition is not a silver bullet for all the questions that you don't have answers to yet. Some of those questions may require active, conscious thinking to generate ideas. The dimension of intuition enables a parallel stream of awareness, which, when coupled with conscious thinking, can give you formidable guidance. This can expedite your journey towards a breakthrough. Being inexplicable, the faculty of intuition exists whether we believe in it or not. It hangs finely on the hinge of our trust.

14. Taking Massive Action

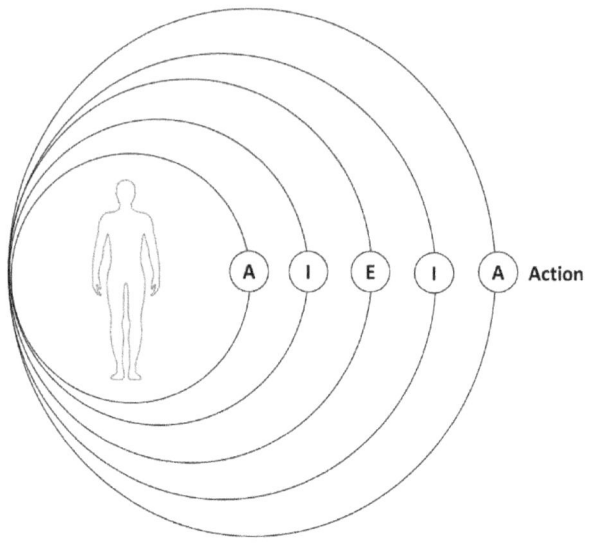

A I E I A Action

The Fifth Dimension

Law of the Land

Galileo Galilei (1564-1642), an Italian astronomer, is considered to be the father of observational astronomy. His work has shaped the field of modern science, and Physics in particular. Galileo studied various elements such as velocity, gravity, motion, etc., and his findings became the basis of further scientific laws and discoveries. One of Galileo's many key works was in the area of motion, which was further built upon by Isaac Newton as the famous three laws. He came up with what we now know as the law of Inertia. Galileo observed what no one else had seen. Galileo derived that objects always have a velocity to them, which leads them to uniform motion. When this velocity is equal to zero, the object is at rest. His second key observation was that objects would resist any change to their motion, which is known as inertia. To put it simply, the law observed that a body in motion would remain in motion unless a force caused it to come to rest. These two observations of Galileo have significant insights hidden in them. These insights can bring immense awareness and help you prepare mentally, as you set forth on the journey for maximum results.

1. The law states that when the velocity of the object is equal to zero, the object is at rest - To get this object to move, a force needs to be applied. And for the object to move, the applied force has to be greater than the inertia. Now, imagine how this law applies to you. The object is the pursuit of your desire, which is at rest right now. For it to move ahead, you need a stimulus, or a force, and that force must be greater than your internal resistance which is holding you back from moving ahead. For you to move ahead, you

need a force significant enough to drive you and your efforts.

2. The law also establishes that objects resist any change to their motion – Your current ways, thoughts, and approach towards achieving your dreams have come into being as a result of your experiences over years. The past failures, fears, and doubts will act as resistance. When you attempt to change some of them, you may face some internal inertia. To move ahead, you need to maneuver through and past this inertia.

You may realize that working on your inertia may not be just a one-time task. Inertia exists inside of us in various forms. You may have to constantly keep a check on it by monitoring your actual progress, as well as your emotional state. When your drive is more than your inertia, you will make progress and move ahead on your plans. But when your drive is just about equal to or less than the inertia, it will seem like things are static.

Point for Reflection

Step 1: Think about the intentions that you have created for your results. Write down these intentions on a piece of paper.

Step 2: List the reasons which have stopped you so far from acting on these intentions in the past.

Step 3: List the possible things which may stop you from acting on your intentions soon.

Step 4: Reflect upon the reasons that may have come up from steps 2 & 3. This is your inertia.

The Field of Forces

In 1936, a book called *Principles of Topological Psychology* hit the stands. The author of the book was Kurt Lewin, a brilliant psychologist who migrated to the UK and then to the USA after Hitler came to power in Germany. Among his many notable works was an equation which later was known as Lewin's equation. The equation stated that behavior was a function of the person and his/her environment.

$$B = f(P, E)$$

The tiny equation set forth an argument that the environment setting had a significant influence on the behavior. Over the last eight-odd decades since Lewin proposed the equation, it has made its existence obvious in our surroundings. We are submerged in waves of information from social media, our lifestyles have become more and more sedentary, our foods have become "faster," and our attention spans have depleted. All these changes, whether good or bad, cannot be attributed to just the environment, as the second variable is the person himself/herself. However, arguably, we have created an environment that influences our behavior, if not controls it. While we looked at the role of inertia of the person in the previous section, it is important to also explore how our environment may help or hinder our efforts. We have to gain insight again from Lewin, for the same.

Lewin proposed a model called "Force Field Analysis," which evaluated forces or factors that influenced a situation. Some forces help the cause and help you move ahead, while some other forces hinder the progress. This resultant tension between the "for" and "against" forces determine the direction of your results. Doing a force field analysis of your external environment can help you identify all the forces at play and help you plan for an effective strategy.

Steps for Conducting a Force Field Analysis:

Step 1: Take a piece of paper and write down your intention at the center of it. E.g. You want to achieve results in the realm of your fitness, and you intend to lose 20 lbs. of weight over the next 4-5 months.

Step 2: Think about all the external environmental factors that may help you in achieving your desired result. E.g. You have a gym nearby your house for you to join, you know a good dietician who can advise you on your diet plans, etc. Once you have thought these through, list these factors one below the other on the left side of the page.

Step 3: Think about all the external environmental factors that may hinder your progress. E.g. Your working hours are rather odd, you don't have much time left for yourself after completing your house chores, etc. Once you have thought these through, list these factors one below the other on the right side of the page.

Step 4: Look at both sides of the forces. Each of these forces should be external and should be relevant to your desired result, i.e. they should have a bearing on your goals.

Step 5: Evaluate the influence of each of the forces listed on both sides on your goals. Rate the level of influence of each factor on a scale of High-Medium-Low. This is a subjective assessment, and there are no right or wrong answers.

Step 6: Glance over the factors and their influence ratings. This analysis will tell you how you stand as of now in terms of the support or resistance you may receive in terms of external conditions.

Step 7: Map out a mitigation strategy to address the forces. Think about which supportive forces you can strengthen and which opposing forces you can weaken. Plan out the actions and get to it.

The First Frontier

In my coaching conversations with professionals, we usually talk about the efforts that have been put in so far towards the achievement of the results. It helps establish a ground zero and identify what all has been tried in the past that did not work and why. Often, I have observed that very little has been done in terms of actions so far. When I explore the reasons for lack of movement, I usually hear responses along the lines of "It is not like I have been delaying it. I was waiting for…" It mostly seems like a perfectly logical explanation of why the wait was prudent and makes complete sense. However, the challenge is that we often wait for the perfect alignment of the stars. We think "If this happens, then I will do it" "If that happens then I will act on it." In the excitement, we wait to have everything line up as we would like it to be. Starting the pursuit itself often becomes the biggest challenge.

I am sure you have heard this fable before. Once a town faced massive floods. A man climbed on the roof of his house to save his life. As the water levels started rising, he prayed to God for help. After some time, a man floating on a raft saw him and shouted, "Come along, we can swim through to safety." The man replied, "Thank you. I am praying to my God and I am sure he will save me." The man on the raft passed by. A little later, another man, rowing his boat, saw him and shouted, "Jump into my boat, I can help you." The response of the stranded man was the same, "Thank you. I am praying to my God and I am sure he will save me." Then a rescue helicopter hovered over the house, and the pilot shouted, "Grab the rope. I will pull you up." The stranded man, waiting for God to help, replied, "Thank you. I am praying to my God and I am sure he will save me." The helicopter, too, went by. The water levels continued to rise, and eventually the stranded man drowned. Upon his death, he confronted God angrily, "I prayed so hard. Why did you not save me?" God replied calmly, "My son, who do you think sent the raft, the boat, and the helicopter?"

Careful planning and evaluation of steps are critical to success; however, endless waiting is detrimental to it. There will never be a time when all forces in your force field will move towards the left side and help you in your pursuits. All the stars may align in your favor, but no one can tell when that will be, if it even were to happen. The world is as perfect as it can be for you to succeed. Don't wait for all the stars to align. We have all heard the quote "The best time to start was yesterday. The second-best time to start is now." Take the first step. Just begin.

Taking action requires us to make choices. Often, we delay the action because we find it difficult to choose, or we are worried that our decision may not be the right one. While a rash decision is not recommended, an endless wait also does not help. We do not give ourselves any margin of error. Our upbringing and societal conditions make us look at every decision as one with binary outcomes: either you win, or you lose. This builds significant pressure to ensure that we don't make a wrong decision. We should always do our due diligence before deciding, however, we should also build a tolerance and understanding for ourselves. Often a wrong action is better than no action. At least it will teach you something. Thomas Edison made 10,000 unsuccessful attempts before perfecting the incandescent electric bulb. Concerning his efforts, he said, "I have not failed. I have just found 10,000 ways that won't work."

Write that email, make that phone call, speak to that one person. Take that one action to get started on your goal. Don't let the thoughts of how you will finish the entire journey overwhelm you. You don't have to complete it all today. All you need to do is begin. Just start, and you will notice that the stars will align themselves.

The Three Hurdles

When it comes to taking action, three elements create the biggest roadblocks. This trio tempts us into inaction. Their allure is very strong and hard to resist. They tend to sneak into our minds effortlessly, like a whiff of air, and hold us back from taking any action. Overcoming their charm requires persistence and discipline, a sort of mental toughness. These three can appear anytime in the journey and one must keep a lookout for them.

1. The "Tomorrow" Syndrome – Have you ever gone back to sleep, turning off the morning alarm, telling yourself that you will start going for a jog tomorrow? Have you ever binged on that pizza or doughnut, telling yourself that you will start your diet tomorrow? Have you ever bought that beautiful dress, telling yourself that you will start saving money tomorrow? We all have

been there, pushing things to tomorrow. Days become weeks, and weeks become months, but that tomorrow never comes. We usually call this tendency to postpone actions, "procrastination." We defer things at will and then reason with ourselves why tomorrow is a better day to act. Over time, the postponing behavior develops itself into a habit, and we surrender ourselves to it. The solution to this challenge lies in a simple equation of cost and benefit. If the cost of taking an action is equal to or more than the perceived benefit, the likelihood of deferment is higher. On the other hand, if the benefits of taking the action significantly outweigh the cost, you are likely to not defer it. You can overcome your tendency to push things to tomorrow by utilizing the same equation that we used to gain an understanding of its reasons. The first way is to make the benefits so appealing to yourself, that the cost of your effort and time looks very small. You can leverage the exercise for visualizing powerful intentions to magnify your desire and need for the same. That should help you overcome the deference. The second way is to work on the opposite. Make the cost of not taking action so high that you are automatically compelled to do it.

2. The "Efficiency" Drive – From power naps to ready-to-eat mixes, our lives run on the tenet of efficiency. We swear by the phrases "bang for the buck" and "no time to waste." We want our lives to be better, but we don't have the time to go through the old trodden way. These needs have led to the rise of the world of "hacks." Nowadays, everything has a hack, a quick and easy shortcut. We have all searched for these easy fixes for something or another. Some people spend hours finding a hack to do something, rather than working on it for a fraction of the time. There is nothing wrong with the notion of efficiency, but it is important to realize that some things take effort. Often, there is no shortcut to success. The hacks may help you, but only to an extent. They may be able to cut down your journey, but only by some miles. Look for smarter ways to do things, but don't rely on just the shortcuts. The way may look longer and tougher, but it will help you build endurance and skills for the future. It will give you the gift of experience and wisdom.

3. The "Not Feeling" Game – "I just don't feel like going to the gym today!" This inner voice can be heard loud and clear on some

days. The general sense amplifies, along with lethargy and the need to take it easy. Sometimes, it may appear that we are at the mercy of our feelings. But the reality is that you can shift your emotional state by shifting your thoughts. The question hounds many people, "What do I do on the days when I don't feel like it?" The unfailing remedy to this is to show up. If you don't feel like doing something on a particular day, don't give in to the temptation. Just get up and show up. You may not do your best work on that day, but you will have made progress. It will still be better than not doing anything at all. When you consistently show up irrespective of how you feel, you set a tone for yourself. This is the "no matter what" spirit which will hold you in good stead.

Making it Just Right

The fairy tale *Goldilocks and the Three Bears* has elicited many interpretations over the last century. The tale is of a young girl named Goldilocks accidentally reaching the house of three bears, where she tries three different bowls of porridge. She tastes all three to find out that she prefers the third bowl of porridge, which is neither too hot nor too cold - It is just right. Many threads of this fairy tale have been depicted in developmental psychology and achievement motivation concepts. One such analogy derived from the Goldilocks story has been that people feel motivated when the challenge they are facing is just right – not too easy that they lose interest nor too difficult that they lose hope. This fine balance in between is the sweet space that triggers the motivation to act.

What can this story imply for you in your pursuit? If you consistently place yourself in this sweet space, you are likely to take massive action. But the question remains how you can do that, especially considering the nature of the results that you have created intentions for. Those are not just any results, but maximum results. How can you make the effort for them just right? The key is to break down the effort into smaller pieces. When you chunk down the task, it makes it seem more manageable and achievable. The level of difficulty does not overwhelm you and becomes just right for you to act. Break your goals down into Goldilocks-sized chunks and then start working on them one step at a time.

The 1% Rule

Plan your actions for the day and review your progress at the end of each day. Reflect upon what worked per your expectations and where you fell short. These reflections will help you mend your ways and identify your actions for tomorrow. The Stoic philosopher Seneca once said, "I will keep constant watch over myself and most usefully will put each day up for review. For this is what makes us evil – that none of us looks back upon our lives. We reflect upon what we are about to do. And yet our plans for the future descend from the past."

When you start taking action, you will realize that no two days are the same. Your effort will vary, and so will the results. There will be some good days, and some will not meet your expectations. Some days will challenge you, and some will test your limits. Don't give up. Keep the 1% rule in mind. It goes like this – Even if you are 1% better than yesterday, you are making progress. Reiterate this to yourself every day.

The 1% rule does not preach that you should be happy with less or no progress. It tells you to stay focused and not give up, even on days when the clouds are looming. Often, we make progress in ways that we don't realize. Every step that you take moves you closer to your result. Keep your intentions in view. Your emotions are the fuel for your actions. The visualization of your intentions will generate the emotional intensity, which will help you find the silver lining amongst the clouds.

Conclusion

John Naisbitt, the bestselling author of *Megatrends*, once said, "The most exciting breakthroughs of the 21st century will not occur because of technology but because of an expanding concept of what it means to be human." As the world around us evolves at a rapid rate, we, too, need to evolve our ways and means. Humans are bestowed with a unique power which has helped our species evolve across the ages of time. It is the power of realization. This book intends to act as the stimulus for that realization. The five dimensions listed in this book require you to invest in building your awareness and capabilities, as well as translate them into persistent effort. Many people aspire for extraordinary results in their life, but surprisingly, very few act on it. You took the effort to read this book, and that is a significant action. You have already initiated your work to manifest the results you desire. And it is a good start.

The pursuit of maximum results is not an easy one. I have noticed that sometimes people jump in to implement the framework with a lot of gusto. But the enthusiasm soon wears off, due to lack of visible results.

While implementing the framework, you may elicit linear results until you hit the inflection point – a space where the breakthrough starts showing its early signs. The inflection point occurs when your efforts across the five dimensions are in absolute alignment with each other. Your thoughts, intentions, feelings, intuition and actions are all working in the same direction for the same cause. That is when maximum results transpire.

Through this book, we explored multiple facets and inner workings of the science of achieving results. I encourage you to explore and experiment. You have five key forces at your disposal:

Your Attention creates focus.
Your Intentions creates resolve.
Your Emotions creates energy.
Your Intuition creates guidance.
And finally, your Actions creates results.

As we come to the close of this book, I invite you to always remind yourself – Abilities can be acquired, beliefs can be instilled, habits can be cultivated, and drive can be energized. All you need is a strong desire and a will to act. As Robert Frost once said, "Do not fear failure but rather fear not trying." Leverage these forces to create massive results because it is not just about the gifts that you have. It is about what you do with them.

Get to work. Your breakthrough is waiting for you.

IF

If you can keep your head when all about you
   Are losing theirs and blaming it on you,
If you can trust yourself when all men doubt you,
   But make allowance for their doubting too;
If you can wait and not be tired by waiting,
   Or being lied about, don't deal in lies,
Or being hated, don't give way to hating,
   And yet don't look too good, nor talk too wise

If you can dream—and not make dreams your
   master;
   If you can think—and not make thoughts your aim;
If you can meet with Triumph and Disaster
   And treat those two impostors just the same;
If you can bear to hear the truth you've spoken
   Twisted by knaves to make a trap for fools,
Or watch the things you gave your life to, broken,
   And stoop and build 'em up with worn-out tools

If you can make one heap of all your winnings
   And risk it on one turn of pitch-and-toss,
And lose, and start again at your beginnings
   And never breathe a word about your loss;
If you can force your heart and nerve and sinew
   To serve your turn long after they are gone,
And so hold on when there is nothing in you
   Except the Will which says to them 'Hold on!'

If you can talk with crowds and keep your virtue,
   Or walk with Kings—nor lose the common touch,
If neither foes nor loving friends can hurt you,
   If all men count with you, but none too much;
If you can fill the unforgiving minute
   With sixty seconds' worth of distance run,
Yours is the Earth and everything that's in it,
   And—which is more—you'll be a Man, my son!

-   Rudiyard Kipling

Did You Enjoy Reading Maximum Results?

Thank you so much for taking the time to read Maximum Results. I truly appreciate it. We have come a long way and I sincerely hope that you enjoyed this journey. It is because of readers like you, that the effort of writing a book becomes worthwhile. I hope that the insights and exercises given in this book help you in achieving maximum results in your life.

I have a favor to ask of you. Can I seek 60 seconds of your time? I would be incredibly grateful and appreciative, if you could write a review for this book on Amazon.

Your words will go a long way in helping me take this book to other readers. More importantly, I would get to know how I was able to help you in your pursuit of maximum results through this book. It would take just a few moments, but it will help me immensely.

Thank you for all your support!

About the Author

Yugesh Mandvikar is an author and a leadership coach. He has been studying human behavior for almost two decades. Over the years, he has extensively coached and consulted individuals and teams on driving high performance and achieving breakthrough results. As an ardent analogist, Yugesh enjoys connecting the dots between seemingly unrelated areas. Apart from having managed portfolios across learning, leadership development, and organization development in global corporations, he has also taught organizational behavior in business schools. Fascinated by the unlimited human capacity, he is on a mission to help one million people achieve their full potential.

Visit www.yugeshmandvikar.com to learn more.

A Note on Attribution of Sources

This book has been a result of extensive literature research. I have tried to attribute the ideas to their sources. However, it is difficult to find the exact source to attribute for some of the fables, legends and quotes. It is possible that I may have made a mistake in either attributing an idea to a wrong source or having missed crediting it. Any such misses are sincerely regretted.